# A STUDY IN
# MILTON'S CHRISTIAN DOCTRINE

# A STUDY IN MILTON'S CHRISTIAN DOCTRINE

BY

ARTHUR SEWELL

ARCHON BOOKS

1967

First published 1939

Reprinted 1967 with permission of
OXFORD UNIVERSITY PRESS
in an unaltered and unabridged edition

Library of Congress Catalog Card Number: 67-26661
Printed in the United States of America

FOR MY
PARENTS

# PREFACE

THIS is very far from an exhaustive account of the development of Milton's Christian doctrine; and I am sure that in some points further thought and research would (and may) show me to be in error. I intend this book as a statement, first, of the way in which I think that development must be studied, and, secondly, of the broad lines on which the relation between Milton's beliefs and the progress and change in his own mind and spirit must be established. My own inquiries have gone as far as two periods of leave from teaching in South Africa and New Zealand have been able to take them.

Reference throughout is made to the Columbia edition of Milton's works.

I am deeply grateful to Mr. W. J. Paylor, who has seen the book through the press. I have also to thank Professor D. Nichol Smith, who advised and encouraged me when this work was in its early state as a B.Litt. thesis, and Professor B. Farrington, who read the typescript and assisted me in many points with his criticism.

ARTHUR SEWELL.

# FOREWORD

AN inquiry into the development of Milton's Christian doctrine must always begin with an attempt to determine the date of the composition of his *De Doctrina Christiana*. And this is a matter of no small difficulty. Sumner,[1] the first editor of the treatise, thought that it was composed in Milton's later years. Mr. Belloc[2] suggests that it was the work of a young mind, and places it somewhere in the sixteen-forties. Professor J. H. Hanford[3] has shown beyond reasonable doubt that Milton's amanuensis, Jeremie Picard, made the fair copy of Book I, chapters xv—end, and of Book II—and presumably also of the earlier chapters of Book I, though these have been lost, and we have only Daniel Skinner's copy of these, made after Milton's death—in the years 1657–60. I have shown reason[4] to suppose that these earlier chapters of Book I were recopied by Daniel Skinner, because they were so much revised and altered that they were in places not easily legible, and that these revisions and alterations were done after Milton had composed the early

---

[1] 'Preliminary Observations to *A Posthumous Treatise on the Christian Doctrine*, etc.', translated by C. R. Sumner, The Prose Works of John Milton, vol. iv, Bohn's Libraries Edition (G. Bell & Sons, London, 1904).

[2] *Milton*, Hilaire Belloc, 'Epilogue on the *De Doctrina*', pp. 287 ff. (Cassell & Co., 1935).

[3] Cf. 'On the Date of Milton's *De Doctrina*', by J. H. Hanford, *Studies in Philology*, 1920, pp. 311–12.

[4] 'Milton's *De Doctrina*', *Essays and Studies of the British Association*, 1933.

books, perhaps Books I—III, of *Paradise Lost*. I
have suggested, too, that these revisions were made
because Milton's thought had changed in certain
important points of doctrine, notably in his views of
the Trinity.

Not only the date, but also the state of the manuscript is of importance. It is not a finished work, for,
as I shall show, there are contradictions in it, which
Milton would hardly have left unresolved if he had
ever made a systematic preparation of the whole
work (as it now stands) for the press.[1] There are
evidences in it of layers of opinion, which tell the
story of the development of Milton's beliefs. We
can see how it was originally determined in form by
those 'shorter manuals' of which Milton speaks in
his preface, and which, he says, were his first study
in the formulation of his system of doctrine. We can
trace his changing view of the Mosaic Law and his
progress to that point where he decided that with the
coming of Christ the whole of the Law was abrogated. We can see that he did not always suppose
that all things were made 'of God'. We can discover
clues to the process by which he enriched his idea of
Gospel Liberty. I consider these points in my first
chapter.

We have to find a place for the treatise in Milton's
spiritual biography. It is not good enough for us to
take the treatise as a fixed point, to which we can
refer the rest of his works and so establish for them a
place in the geography of his ideas. The treatise is
no more a fixed point than any other of his works.

[1] The manuscript of *De Doctrina Christiana* is now to be found
in the Public Record Office (S.P. 9.63).

They help us to explain it just as much as it helps us to understand them. We must accommodate them to it no more and no less than we must accommodate it to them. There must be no accommodation: we have to see the treatise and the other works in their setting within the whole of Milton's spirit. And this especially applies in our attempt to understand the relation between the treatise and *Paradise Lost*. Because in *De Doctrina Christiana* Milton set down what he thought to be true, we must not suppose that he always set it down with the sincerity of his whole spirit. That sincerity is reported under more favourable conditions and perhaps more truly in *Paradise Lost* and the other poems.

To discover the setting of the treatise in the development of Milton's mind and heart, we must see how far his attitude to God, his affection towards God, is illustrated in the earlier works. Two things emerge from a reading of the earlier works, particularly the prose works. First, Milton's clear statements that his spirit was early dedicated to God cannot be accepted without reserve. Rather does he seem to have dedicated God to the needs of his own spirit. He takes God for granted and he takes for granted, too, that God is specially favourable to him and to his own people. Secondly, Milton's view of liberty in these earlier works is restricted to the natural plane. He makes verbal tribute to the supernatural element in Gospel Liberty, but this element is never decisive and is never fully integrated with the immediate needs and the persuasiveness of his argument. In his deepest nature, he still thinks of freedom in psychological terms, and he makes his best points from his view of man as psychologically and politically, not spiritually, free. It is only in 1659, when he came to write *A Treatise of Civil Power in Ecclesiastical Causes*, that the supernatural aspect of Gospel Liberty begins to determine the logic of his view. I elaborate this impression of Milton's earlier views of God and Liberty in my third chapter.

*Paradise Lost*, at least in the first three or four books, seems to me to represent an earlier state of opinion than *De Doctrina Christiana*, and I give reasons for this view in the opening sections of my fourth chapter. It is more important, however, to observe that there is one sense in which the treatise and the poem are to be regarded as activities of Milton's mind and spirit at one and the same stage of their development. Both give evidence that Milton is searching for God, for some way of justifying God's ways with men. There is in both the signs of the troubled spirit and the perplexed mind. The treatise shows Milton apparently reaching some settlement in the intellectual system of his doctrine. While it may be difficult to make a related whole of all the various elements of belief, expounded in *De Doctrina Christiana*, Milton certainly seems to have satisfied himself, very often in unorthodox fashion, that his search was completed in many particulars. Is this enough? Did the treatise satisfy, not only his mind, but also his whole spirit? Did it even satisfy his mind? I think not. His mind seems to me to have many times gone its own way, to have lost its anchorage in his deepest nature, to have ceased to correspond with the needs of his inmost spirit. While the treatise reports a part of the man, his mind, the later poems, *Paradise Lost*, *Paradise Regained*, and *Samson Agonistes*, seem to me to report a different, a more fundamental part, perhaps in many places the whole man. What Milton really believed, then (if I may use the phrase), may be something different from the doctrine argued in *De Doctrina Christiana*. This is the conclusion to which I come in the later chapters of this book.

# CONTENTS

# I

## THE TREATISE ON CHRISTIAN DOCTRINE

### I

IN the preface to *De Doctrina Christiana*, Milton gives us some account of the stages in which his treatise on doctrine was compiled, and he makes it clear that his religious views underwent a continual process of revision over a period of years.

While he was still a young man, he entered upon an 'assiduous course of study',

> beginning with the books of the Old and New Testaments in their original languages, and going diligently through a few of the shorter systems of divines, in imitation of whom I was in the habit of classing under certain heads whatever passages of Scripture occurred for extraction, to be made use of hereafter as occasion might require. (xiv. 5.)

These 'shorter systems of divines' are named in Edward Phillips's life of Milton. Edward Phillips there records that

> the *Sunday's* work was for the most part the Reading each day a Chapter of the *Greek* Testament, and hearing his Learned Exposition upon the same. . . . The next work after this, was the writing from his own dictation, some part, from time to time, of a Tractate which he thought fit to collect from the ablest of Divines, who had written of that Subject: *Amesius,*

I

*Wollebius*, etc., *viz.* A perfect System of Divinity, of which more hereafter.

Unfortunately, Edward Phillips forgot that he had promised to say 'more hereafter' of this system of divinity. Had he remembered, we might have been saved from the hazards of much conjecture.

Milton was not the man to be content with extracts even from the 'ablest' of contemporary theologians. It was the very centre of his protestantism that

> no man, no synod, no session of men, though called the church, can judge definitely the sense of scripture to another man's conscience.

This he called the 'general maxim of the protestant religion'. Certainly it was the maxim of his own inquiries into Christian doctrine, and the second stage in the composition of his treatise was an independent attempt to make out of the Bible 'some methodical tractate of Christian doctrine'.

> I deemed it therefore safest and most advisable to compile for myself, by my own labour and study, some original treatise which should always be at hand, derived solely from the word of God itself. (xiv. 7.)

In this labour, Milton persevered diligently for several years ('aliquot annos'). It then became clear to him that much that he had accepted as true and proper doctrine needed to be re-examined and reshaped in the light of his reading of scripture. More than he was aware of still remained, he wrote, which required to be more rigidly examined by the rule of Scripture, and reformed after a more accurate model. (xiv. 9.)

This re-examination was the third stage in the compilation of *De Doctrina Christiana*.

It is an extremely difficult matter to give an approximate date to each of these three stages. Milton undertook the education of his two nephews soon after his return from Italy in 1639. In 1640, then, it is likely that he was already occupied with the first stage, 'the dictation of a tractate from the ablest of divines' or (as Milton puts it) 'going through the shorter systems of divines'. Apart from this, the only other date for which we have authority is taken from the life of Milton which was probably written by his other nephew, John. The writer of this life tells us that among the works which Milton 'began' when he was excused from 'attending in his office of Secretary'—that is, in 1655 —was 'the framing of a *Body of Divinity* out of the Bible'. He goes on to say that this work, together with *Paradise Lost* and a Latin Thesaurus, 'hee finish'd after the Restoration'. In the next paragraph, with *Paradise Regained* and *Samson Agonistes* also in mind, he added:

> In these Works, and the instruction of some Youth or other at the intreaty of his friends, hee in great Serenity spent his time & expir'd no less calmly in the Yeare 1674.

We have to turn to the manuscript of *De Doctrina Christiana*, now in the Public Record Office. The

treatise was obviously first copied out fairly and, to
some extent, ornamentally by one of Milton's
amanuenses, identified by Professor J. H. Hanford
as Jeremie Picard.[1]   Picard was in Milton's service
from about 1656 until some years after the Restoration, and we can be sure that this version of *De
Doctrina Christiana* was written while Milton had
*Paradise Lost* very much in mind or (as I think)
while the poem was actually being composed.

Fourteen chapters in Picard's hand have been lost
—or seem to have been lost, for the first fourteen
chapters of the treatise are in the hand of Daniel
Skinner, who was Milton's pupil and amanuensis in
the closing years of his life.  Skinner prepared the
work for the press in what seems to have been a very
roundabout way.  For chapter xiv (pp. 183–96) he
used a smaller sheet than he had in the first thirteen
chapters, and this sheet conforms roughly in size to
those in the remainder of the manuscript.  Further,
unlike the earlier chapters, but like the ones later, it
had been paginated independently, and the numbers
were struck out when the whole work was paginated
consecutively.   It would seem that Skinner wrote
this fourteenth chapter before he made his fair copy
of the first thirteen.  His procedure may have been
something like this: he first of all prepared the work
for the press by rewriting only those passages (or
chapters) made most illegible by the many alterations and additions with which Jeremie Picard's
part of the manuscript is disfigured; he then decided

---

[1] Cf. 'On the Date of Milton's *De Doctrina*', by J. H. Hanford,
in *Studies in Philology*, 1920, pp. 311–12.   I accept Professor
Hanford's account of the work of this amanuensis.

to copy out the whole work in his neat Italian hand; and when he came to chapter xiv, already fairly copied, he may have decided (for the labour was proving arduous) that the rest of the work could easily be read by the printer. Whether this conjecture is right or not, it is reasonable to suppose that Skinner was prompted to copy out the first thirteen chapters because the manuscript was much amended and supplemented and less easily legible than the rest of the work. It is significant that these early chapters contain Milton's most startling departures from orthodox opinion.

The manuscript of *De Doctrina Christiana* seems to show two stages, the second and the third, in the development of Milton's belief. We have Jeremie Picard's fair copy, doubtless prepared by Milton as a guide for the composition of *Paradise Lost*. We have, too, the evidence of development and change of mind, contained in the revisions and additions made to this copy in Book I, chapters xv—the end, and in Book II. These revisions show that Milton at least to some extent 'reshaped' his doctrine after Picard had made his copy. How much of this reshaping was done in the first fourteen chapters the manuscript unfortunately bears no witness.

We can give a *terminus a quo* for the date of certain chapters in what I have called the second stage of the composition of the treatise. At least one element in the doctrine expounded in *De Doctrina Christiana* has become settled in Milton's mind after he wrote *A Treatise of Civil Power in Ecclesiastical Causes*, published in 1659. *De Doctrina Christiana* states unequivocally, in passages written by Picard, that the whole of the Mosaic Law was abolished with the coming of Christ. (xvi. 125.) In *A Treatise of Civil Power*, Milton declares that it is still a matter of some doubt whether the law contained in the tables was abrogated by Christ. It is clear that Milton's mind was busy with the problem; it is clear, too, that he had not finally resolved it. Certain chapters of *De Doctrina Christiana*, therefore, must have been composed in or after 1659; and Milton was engaged in the compilation of his treatise while *Paradise Lost* was in process of composition.

If we suppose, then, that the second stage of the composition of the treatise must be dated about 1658–60, the third stage—the process of revision and 'reshaping'—must have taken place after the Restoration. To determine more accurately at what time this was, we must compare the doctrine in the treatise with the thought which lies behind *Paradise Lost*. This will be my concern later in this book. Such a comparison should show, also, whether the elements of doctrine argued in the first fourteen chapters were established during this process of revision or were accepted by Milton while *Paradise Lost* was being composed. It is important to point out, however, that the state of the manuscript in the Public Record Office warns us not to study *Paradise Lost* too confidently in the light of *De Doctrina Christiana*. We should be on the look-out, not only for evidences of agreement, but also for signs of development and change.

One more point must be made before we leave the consideration of Daniel Skinner's dealings with the manuscript. It has been assumed that Milton withheld the treatise from publication on account of the heterodox views stated within it. And it is true that Milton would have committed a statutory offence if he had published the work during the years of the Commonwealth and, indeed, of the Restoration. This would not necessarily have deterred him, and there is some evidence, at least, that the delay in the publication of the treatise was not due to any reluctance on his part, prompted by a fear of prosecution.

Milton declared boldly in the preface:

> I readily give as wide a circulation as possible to what I esteem my best and richest possession. (xiv. 9.)

And a little later:

> Concealment is not my object; it is to the learned that I address myself. (xiv. 11.)

He certainly intended the treatise to be published when he wrote his preface, and he was conscious of the fact that many things in it might give offence. But, as he says, concealment was not his object.

Daniel Skinner, in whose care Milton left the work, together with the Letters of State, thought that no prejudice might accrue to him if he saw the work through the press. The author of the 'anonymous' life, perhaps John Phillips, who knew a good deal of Milton's later years, mentions the 'speculative points, differing perhaps from that commonly receiv'd,' to be found in *De Doctrina Christiana*, and he adds that this 'is thought to bee the reason that never was printed'. He had heard of this reason at second-hand, and could not say for certain why the book was withheld from the press. Since he obviously knows a good deal about Milton's later years, this is most probably a reference to Skinner's dealings with the work, not Milton's. We know for a fact that Skinner withdrew the treatise from the press because of the speculative points and the prejudice that might 'accrue' to him on account of publishing them.

Why did Milton change his mind after the preface was written? He is bold enough there: why did he become timid ? There seem to be three possibilities. First, Milton may have been better advised after the preface was written, and he may have put the work aside for fear of the consequences of publication. Secondly, the treatise may possibly have occupied Milton until the last years of his life, so that he had no time before his death to prepare it for the press. Thirdly, Milton may have changed his mind about publication for some reason other than the fear of prosecution, even though the work was ready for the press. He may, in fact, have begun to doubt the truth or, at least, the importance of his own conclusions.

The simplest hypothesis would suggest that the preface, composed after the completion of the work, was written just before the Restoration. It seems probable that under the Commonwealth, Milton would be ready to assume that his work, notwithstanding the heterodox opinions, would 'meet with a candid reception from all parties'. When his political opponents were in the ascendancy, however, it was natural that he should refrain from giving further occasion for persecution by the public statement of his religious views. The treatise, therefore, was reluctantly put aside, and Milton decided to withhold it from the press. This view receives some support from Milton's last prose pamphlet, *Of True Religion, Heresie, Schism and Toleration*, published in 1673. There he seems to have had *De Doctrina Christiana* in mind, when he wrote:

> At least then let them have leave to write in Latin which the common people understand not; that what they hold may be discust among the Learned only. (vi. 178.)

On the face of it, the whole of this pamphlet reads very much like a plea for the publication of Milton's treatise.

Certain other considerations seem to me to weigh against this hypothesis. The physical state of the manuscript suggests a process of revision lasting for a period of years. The disagreements in doctrine between the treatise and *Paradise Lost* are so important that it seems unlikely that the treatise was completed in time to serve as a doctrinal guide in the composition of the poem. On certain points, the treatise (so it seems to me) must be regarded as the argument of opinions which are not fully formed in *Paradise Lost*, but which Milton was led to adopt during the very process of poetical composition. Further, *Paradise Regained, Samson Agonistes*, and *Of True Religion* seem to me to shadow a mind not quite so confident as that expressed in the preface to the treatise, not quite so certain that matter of belief has been sifted from matter of opinion. They seem, indeed, to indicate that Milton may have withheld his treatise from the press at least partly because his search was not ended. In this view, then, Milton examined the Scriptures to a point where he seemed settled in his faith and established in those points, 'not commonly receiv'd': so settled and established, indeed, that he wrote his preface to the work. There was delay in publication, perhaps due to the hostile temper of those in power. The delay was fortunate, for Milton became a little more humble about his conclusions, and was persuaded, indeed, that their importance was not necessary to salvation.

*Of True Religion* may be a plea for the publication of *De Doctrina Christiana*. Its temperate references to beliefs, foreign to Milton's own, suggest to me another motive. They read like the words of a man, not wholly self-assured in argument, anxious to consider and understand the fruits of other minds, still open to new convictions. Milton, perhaps, still wanted to publish his treatise, but no longer as the last word.

To elucidate this hypothesis by an examination of the development of Milton's religious views is the purpose of this study.

## II

*De Doctrina Christiana* developed piecemeal. It began as a compilation of passages taken from the 'shorter systems of divines', notably Ames and Wollebius. It still retains the form (and much of the matter) of the manuals of these two theologians,

*Medulla Theologiae*, by William Ames (1576–1633), and *Christianae Theologiae Compendium* (1637), by Johan Wolleben or Wollebius (1586–1629). It is a patchwork thing, never conceived as a whole, an orthodox body of doctrine, altered, deleted, and amended as Milton's views changed. It is like a suit of clothes, made to fit a young man, taken in here, and let out there, as the cloth wears thin and the young man's figure alters with the years.

The treatise itself affords indisputable evidence of its own development. This evidence is of two kinds. In some instances, Milton's earlier thought still lies embedded in the text; and many alterations and revisions record the progress and change of Milton's views. There is, too, a third kind of evidence, the evidence of significant omissions. The most notable of these is Milton's evident lack of interest in the figure of Satan in the treatise. Ames, in his *Medulla*, devotes considerable space to a description of the Temptation of Adam and Eve, and Milton's account of the Fall in *Paradise Lost* seems to owe a good deal to Ames. It is reasonable to suppose that an earlier state of Milton's treatise made fuller mention of the Devil, and that this has been omitted and cancelled in the version we have to-day. To understand the development of the treatise, then, we have to take into account these three kinds of evidence.

Milton does not seem to have gone through the treatise with a view to deleting and altering all those statements which conflict with his changed opinion. There are contradictions within the work which themselves show different stages in the process of change.

In chapter iv, 'Of Predestination', Milton used these words:

> This [i.e. that the general decree of election is personally applicable to each particular believer] is most explicitly declared by the whole of Scripture, which offers salvation and eternal life equally to all, under the condition of obedience in the Old Testament, and of faith in the New. (xiv. 107.)

When he wrote that, he clearly believed that it was part of God's covenant that, before the coming of Christ, the Jews at least could be saved by obedience to the Law. This view is in conflict with the later, more rational, view that 'Jews and others, who lived before Christ, and many also who have lived since his time, but to whom he has never been revealed, should be saved by faith in God alone'. (xv. 349.) And, indeed, in chapter iv, two pages later than the passage quoted above, Milton seems to prepare for this later view in a parenthesis which reads very much like an addition to the text:

> (for in the Old Testament scarcely a single expression can be discovered referring to election properly so called; that is, election to eternal life). (xiv. 113.)

There is another similar contradiction in the treatise, illustrating the change in Milton's attitude to the Law. In chapter x, 'Of the Special Government of Man', Milton's discussion of divorce leads him to consider what the law of Moses has to say about it. He is concerned to show that ' hardness of heart' was never the sole or principal reason for the enactment of that law whereby a man was allowed to put away his wife. The whole of the civil law, he says, was given because of the hardness of men's hearts, but that does not mean that it was 'wrongfully' or 'improperly' given. Nor does it mean that Christ therefore abrogated the legitimate use of it. Christ, Milton declares, 'does not abrogate the law itself'. Just as positively he adds:

> In this sense almost the whole of the civil law might be said to have been given on account of the hardness of their hearts; whence St. Paul reproves the brethren, 1 Cor. vi. 6. because they had recourse to it, though no one argues from hence that the civil law is, or ought to be abrogated. (xv. 169.)

This was not, of course, his final view. His doctrine of Gospel Liberty led him to the belief that nothing, not even the Ten Commandments, could stand under the gospel as a prescription to man's conscience. No shred of the Law remains obligatory on the believer. Nothing is obligatory, for, if it were, man would still be servile, still in his pupillage. That the Christian may be free, the whole of the civil law as well as the ceremonial must be regarded as abrogated:

> On the introduction of the gospel, or new covenant through faith in Christ, the whole of the preceding covenant, in other words the entire Mosaic law, was abolished. (xvi. 125.)

Milton's earlier Trinitarian belief is indicated in one passage still remaining in the text of *De Doctrina*

*Christiana.* In chapter ix, 'Of the Special Government of Angels', Milton is anxious to refute the common belief that Michael is Christ. He quotes Rev. xii. 7, 8, in which Jude says of Michael: 'When contending with the devil he disputed about the body of Moses, he durst not bring against him a railing accusation'. Milton adds this comment:

> which would be an improper expression to use with reference to Christ, especially if he be God (*praesertim Deo*). (xv. 105.)

But in chapter v, Milton has been at great pains to show that the Son cannot possibly be regarded as God supreme, and there is, of course, never any doubt that the Son is God. This phrase, then—*praesertim Deo*—must be a relic from the time when Milton was still in some doubt about the Trinity, and this part of the treatise, at least, must have been composed before Milton reached with any assurance his anti-Trinitarian view.

In the treatise Milton argues with great force that the world was created *ex Deo*, and that therefore the substance of the world can never be destroyed. Not even God, Milton claims, can annihilate the world's substance, for, if he did, he would annihilate his own substance. In chapter v, 'Of the Son of God', he wrote:

> For to Adam God stood less in the relation of Father, than of Creator, having only formed him from the dust of the earth; whereas he was properly the Father of the Son made of his own substance. (xiv. 187.)

Here the 'dust of the earth' is opposed to God's 'own substance'. It is possible, perhaps, to reconcile this passage with the view *omnia ex Deo* by arguing that Milton is claiming that Adam was created 'mediately', the Son 'immediately'. The opposition seems to me to be too pointed for that reconciliation to be made. It seems much more likely that when Milton wrote these words, he held the view expounded by Wollebius in his *Compendium*; namely, that the world was made partly out of nothing, partly out of 'matter naturally inert', a species of dust, in which was no life and no disposition until the Creator so worked upon it.[1] In a later chapter, Milton plainly shows that at one stage of the composition of the treatise he did not believe that all things are of God. When he speaks of the final conflagration, he considers whether or not the substance of the world shall be destroyed. He concludes:

> Whether by this [i.e. the final conflagration] is meant the destruction of the substance of the world itself, or only a change in the nature of its constituent parts, is uncertain, and of no importance to determine. (xvi. 369.)

What must we then conclude ? That when the treatise was first composed Milton had not reached the view—*omnia ex Deo*; and that chapter vi was either written or at least wholly revised after Milton had compiled the last chapter in Book I, as we have it to-day.

[1] Wollebius, *Compendium Theologiae*, editio novissima, 1648, p. 30.

### III

The additions and alterations to the manuscript of *De Doctrina Christiana* are of four kinds. First, Milton very often confirms his earlier thought by the addition of a passage from scripture and a further comment. Secondly, he sometimes adds a comment and a passage from scripture, which not merely confirm the earlier thought but also exhibit a change of emphasis or a new interest. Thirdly, further proof of an earlier position is discovered in some new relation to other elements in Milton's belief, expounded elsewhere—in two instances, expounded in one of the first fourteen chapters. Lastly, Milton sometimes changes his mind or resolves a doubt.

The passages in which Milton confirms his earlier thought have a real significance, for they are evidence of those points of doctrine in which Milton was chiefly interested. They stress for us those ideas which were central in his belief. There are large sections of the treatise in which nothing is added, nothing is amended. In view of the revisions made elsewhere, we can assume that these sections no longer occupied Milton's mind after the first draft of the treatise had been made. For example, the Second Book, *Of the Worship of God*, concerning our duties towards God and man, has been amended in very few places. Milton seems to have stood fast in his view of 'Love, or the Worship of God'. It was in his conception of Faith, or 'the knowledge of God', that his mind remained so long unsatisfied.

One or two examples of the merely confirmatory passages will be sufficient.

Milton emphasizes the view that Faith rests ultimately, not on Christ, but on God—an orthodox view which is to be found in Ames's *Medulla*, but to which Milton must later have given a special meaning in view of his anti-Trinitarian position. In confirmation of his statement in chapter xx,

> the ultimate object of faith is not Christ the Mediator, but God the Father. (xv. 403.)

Milton has later added this all-important passage from John xii. 44:

> qui credit in me non credit in me sed in eum qui misit me.

> he that believeth on me, believeth not on me, but on him that sent me. (xv. 402–3.)

Faith, for Milton, was that knowledge of God which enables a man to live the good life 'through the guidance of the spirit of truth'. In chapter xxvii, he has added to the manuscript a passage from the Epistle to the Romans which seems to me to epitomize the conclusion to which his thought everywhere tends.

> . . . present your bodies . . . a reasonable service; and be not conformed to this world; but be ye transformed by the renewing of your mind, that ye may prove what is that good and acceptable and perfect will of God. (xvi. 155.)

2

On this view of Gospel Liberty Milton could rest. It was surely in the mood in which this paragraph was added that Milton wrote his *Paradise Regained*.

It is important, in Milton's view, that Christ died, not merely for 'many', but for all. He sought to demonstrate this in chapter xvi, 'Of the Ministry of Redemption', by citing a number of passages from the Bible. He quoted Eph. i. 10, 'that he might gather together in one all things in Christ, both which are in heaven, and which are on earth'. In the margin of the manuscript, this most emphatic comment has been added:

> Tam ergo in terra sine exceptione omnia quam in Coelis.
>
> all things therefore on earth without a single exception, as well as in heaven. (xv. 318–19.)

Milton's exposition of the nature of Faith and of Gospel Liberty would not have been nearly so satisfactory had he not amended and added to his first statement. Perhaps the most significant addition made in this connexion is to be found at the beginning of chapter xviii, 'Of Regeneration'. This passage has been added in a later hand:

> Supernaturalis renovationis ratio, non solum naturales hominis facultates recte nimirum intelligendi libereque volendi plenius adhuc restituit, sed etiam internum praesertim hominem quasi novum creat, novasque etiam facultates supernaturales renovatorum mentibus divinitus infuntit.
>
> The intent of supernatural renovation is not only to restore man more completely than before to the use of his natural faculties, as regards his power to form right

judgement, and to exercise free will; but to create afresh, as it were, the inward man, and infuse from above new and supernatural faculties into the minds of the renovated. (xv. 366–7.)

This addition is the fuller explanation of an amendment which has been made in the previous chapter. When the treatise was first compiled, he had divided the 'modes of renovation', that is, the stages by which man comes to faith in God, into two —'external' and 'internal'. The 'external' mode seems to have been that by which man undergoes a merely psychological change and makes acknowledgement that God, through Christ, has opened up for him the way to salvation. The 'internal' mode was described by Milton, a little dubiously, in a passage which was later cancelled. This passage points out that the 'internal' mode is hardly distinguishable from regeneration itself. A better distinction, however, occurred to him later. He deleted the two words *externa* and *interna*, and substituted the words *naturalis* and *supernaturalis*. The change of thought plainly appears. For a threefold process of regeneration, Milton substituted a simpler and more acceptable twofold process. Man, first, through penitence, through 'hearing of' and 'hearkening to' God, finds that his natural mind and will are partially renewed or at least turned Godward. But true regeneration itself is 'supernatural' and the 'inward man' is created 'afresh', the 'old man being destroyed'. This distinction between the 'natural' and the 'supernatural' was highly important in the edifice of Milton's belief.

When the treatise was first dictated, Milton seems to have laid insufficient emphasis on the freedom of the will and the renewal of that freedom through grace. We find him adding in a number of places the statement that the will as well as the mind is renewed. It was, indeed, necessary to Milton's thought that the renovation of man should not only involve an enlightenment of the mind, but also a quickening of his will. For the end of faith is good works, freely willed out of an understanding of spiritual things. 'Freely willed'—for Milton freedom is the condition of value.

So, in his discussion of Renovation, Milton had first written of the change which comes over the renewed man:

> Haec, quoniam a Deo est *illuminatio* vocatur.
>
> Inasmuch as this change is from God, those in whom it takes place are said to be enlightened. (xv. 354–5.)

To this he later added these words:

> et *velle datum.*

which Sumner translates as:

> and to be endued with power to will what is good;

but which, in view of Milton's whole thought, may be more simply translated:

> and to be endued with the power of free-will.

Two lines earlier, the words, 'voluntas aliqua ex parte renovata' ('the will of man being partially renewed') have been added to Milton's general description of the fruits of man's renovation.

That Milton was specially concerned to lay emphasis on this renewal of the will is further proved by another addition to the manuscript in the same chapter. He points out that even the weakest of man's efforts may be ascribed to the power of God working within him and he quotes Phil. ii. 12, 13:

> work out your own salvation with fear and trembling; for it is God worketh in you both to will and to do of his good pleasure. (xv. 356–7.)

After this passage, the following striking comment has been added in a later hand:

> Quid hoc aliud est nisi efficere in nobis libere agere, quod lapsi antea non potuimus nisi vocati ac restituti ? neque enim efficitur in nobis velle, quin libere quoque agere simul efficiatur, quandoquidem haec libertas ipsum esse voluntatis est.

> This can only imply that he works in us the power of acting freely, of which, since our fall, we were incapable, except by means of a calling and renewal. For the power of volition cannot be wrought in us, without the power of free agency being at the same time imparted; since it is in this power that the will itself consists.

This view is further developed when Milton considers exhortations to repentance. In another addition to his treatise, he declares that such exhortations can only be made to men in whom the will has been at least partially enfranchised:

Hortatio autem omnis frustra adhiberetur, nisi homini-
bus naturali saltem hac renovatione aliquem in modum
affectis, id est, aliquo mentis judicio atque arbitrii
libertate praeditis.

All exhortation, however, would be addressed in vain to
such as were not in some measure renewed, at least in
the natural mode here described; that is to say, who were
not endued with some portion of mental judgement and
liberty of will. (xv. 360–1.)

In the chapters on Renovation and Regeneration,
Milton's thought becomes bolder and more original
with these later additions to the treatise. By means
of them, indeed, he is able to bring new meaning
into language largely taken over from the 'shorter
systems of divines', new meaning too to the Scriptures. His passion for freedom, his belief that
individual responsibility is alone compatible with
human dignity, inspires each word of them.

IV

The most important new development in Milton's
thought, shown in the revised portions of the
treatise, concerned the abrogation of the Mosaic
Law and the more exact description of Gospel
Liberty. The view that the Law was totally abrogated has as a corollary the view that it was intended
for the Israelites alone. A number of changes in the
treatise show that Milton progressively reduced the
scope of the Law as much as possible. The description of the Law now reads:

Lex Mosaica erat multorum præceptorum, Israelitis
duntaxat, scripta institutio.

The Mosaic Law was a written code consisting of many precepts, intended for the Israelites alone. (xvi. 102–3.)

The word *duntaxat* has been added in the margin as a substitute for the word *potissimum* ('chiefly') cancelled in the body of the text. The paragraph expounding and illustrating the phrase *Israelitis duntaxat* has also been added in the margin in a later hand. This paragraph emphasizes the importance of the wall of division between Gentiles and the Jews, and prepares us for certain other revisions later in the chapter, in which Milton suggests that the law of nature fulfils for the Gentiles the same purpose as the Mosaic Law for the Jews. Where he had first written:

> Hinc non Judaeis modo sed omnibus et immo non regenitis lex data est, etsi non plane Mosaica.

> Hence not only for the Jews but also for all those who are not yet regenerate was the law given, but not the full Mosaic Law,

we now read:

> Hinc omnibus nondum regenitis lex naturae; data est in eundem finem atque data est Israelitis lex Mosaica.

> Hence to those who are not yet regenerate, the law of nature has the same obligatory force, and is intended to serve the same purposes, as the law of Moses to the Israelites. (xvi. 108–9.)

It was part of Milton's view that God, through the law of nature, calls us and holds us responsible for every moment of conduct, even though we be unregenerate. His analogy between the Law of

Moses and the law of nature illuminates for us his view of the way in which man may become reconciled with God.

Milton was anxious, too, to reduce the rewards of obedience to the Law and to restrict the promise of eternal life to those who live in a knowledge of spiritual things. After all, if he argues (as he does) that many, Jews and others, to whom Christ has not been revealed, may be saved by faith in God alone, the importance of the Law is considerably diminished and the Covenant of the Law becomes, indeed, a mere 'schoolmaster' to bring us to Christ, as St. Paul described it. And I imagine that for Milton the law of nature was the better and more convincing schoolmaster. This whittling down of the importance of the Law is apparent in many other alterations in the manuscript of the treatise.

When Milton first commented on the words—'a promise of life to such as should keep it and a curse on such as should be disobedient'—which occur in the description of the Mosaic Law, he saw no need to modify it. Later, however, he returned to it and added these words:

> Huius nimirum non aeternae ut Lev. xxvi. toto capite apparet.

> namely, temporal life, as is obvious from the whole of the twenty-sixth chapter of Leviticus. (xvi. 106–7.)

This had to be further modified in view of Milton's belief that many, even in the Old Testament, may be saved by faith in God. This modification is found in a later addition to the treatise:

Vitam autem aeternam etsi lex non promittit, prophetae tamen sic innuere videntur.

Though the law, however, does not promise eternal life, this latter seems to be implied in the language of the prophets. (xvi. 106–7.)

And the meaning of this is revealed by a change made later in the same chapter. Milton had originally written:

lex etiam per fidem justificavit sed non sine operibus legis.

the law even justified through faith but not without the works of the law.

This has been changed to:

Sub lege, etiam per fidem justificabantur homines Deo fidentes, sed non sine operibus legis.

Under the law, those who trusted in God were justified by faith indeed, but not without the works of the law. ( xvi. 150–1.)

And Milton's last and most rational word on this topic is contained in the addition of a brief sentence which seems to be informed with all Milton's passionate distrust of a merely external obedience, an obligatory service:

*Littera occidit,* id est, Littera Legis sive *Elementum,* ut alias dicitur; *occidit,* id est, vitam aeternam non promisit.

" the letter killeth," that is, the letter of the law (elsewhere called " the elements "), " killeth," in other words, does not promise eternal life. (xvi. 110–11.)

The emphasis on the responsibility of the individual and the dubious importance of all external disciplines in the life of the believer led Milton, in his revision of the treatise, to a further depreciation of the significance of the sacraments. Several additions and alterations in the manuscript seem to be witnesses of Milton's growing consciousness of the relative futility of all merely outward shows. At the beginning of the discussion of the sacraments, Milton first of all referred to the 'sealing' (*obsignatio*) of the Covenant of Grace. He later added:

> vel potius per externa quaedam signa repraesentatio.
>
> or rather of its representation under certain outward shows. (xvi. 164–5.)

Milton makes it clear that he took what has been called a 'Receptionist' attitude to the sacraments; that is to say, the sacrament only had efficacy for those who took part in it 'with a sincere heart'. The words—*sincero animo proposito*—have been added to his description of sacraments in general. To his account of the Passover he has later added the sentence:

> eiusque sanguinis aspersi efficacia ad salutem eis qui festum illud puro corde celebrarent.
>
> and the efficacy of the sprinkling of his blood for the salvation of such as celebrated the feast with purity of heart. (xvi. 168–9.)

Those who are to be baptized, we are told in another addition to the manuscript, must 'engage themselves to pureness of life'. Baptism is, indeed, a vow, an engagement on the part of man in response to a promise on the part of God. It is doubtful, Milton concludes in still another addition, whether baptism is not meant for proselytes alone.

There are two other added passages which seem to show with what profound feeling Milton's contempt of outward shows was accompanied. They show, too, the fervour with which Milton despised and denounced anything 'papistical', anything that seemed to him to savour of superstition. These additions are made to his discussion of the Lord's Supper, and they are the only passage in which he departs from the unemotional argumentation which is the general manner of the work. In the first addition, he protests that if it is indeed Christ's 'literate flesh' which is eaten in the Mass, 'the consequence would be that the very worst of the communicants, to say nothing of the mice and worms by which the eucharist is occasionally devoured, would through the virtue of this heavenly bread attain eternal life'. (xvi. 195.) The second addition is even more forceful:

> Lastly, in the Mass the sacred body of Christ, after having completed its appointed course of hardship and suffering, is dragged back from its state of exaltation at the right hand of the Father to a condition even more wretched and degrading than before; it is again exposed to be broken, and crushed, and bruised by the teeth not only of men, but of brutes; till, having passed through the whole process of digestion, it is cast out at length into the draught; a profanation too horrible to be even alluded to without shuddering. (xvi. 213.)

There is here much of the venom and angry contempt of the old controversialist. The writing is enriched by it: we wonder whether there was special occasion for it.

V

The first fourteen chapters of the treatise were fairly copied for the press by Daniel Skinner, and in these chapters Milton argues his anti-Trinitarian position. The only passage in the rest of the work which plainly shows his unorthodox view of the Trinity is an addition to the manuscript in a later hand. In the discussion of Christ's satisfaction, Milton has added these words to the sentence in which he rejects the Socinian view:

> hoc tamen fateor, me non videre quo pacto qui filium eiusdem cum Patre essentiae esse volunt; eius vel incarnationem, vel satisfactionem possint satis expedire.

> At the same time I confess myself unable to perceive how those who consider the Son as of the same essence with the Father, can explain either his incarnation, or his satisfaction. (xv. 319.)

It seems unlikely that this relation between the view that the Son and the Father are not of the same essence and the nature of Christ's incarnation would only have occurred to Milton as an afterthought. It seems still more unlikely that no part of the argument in the last nineteen chapters of Book I would involve the mention of his anti-Trinitarianism, if he had indeed been anti-Trinitarian when those chapters were written. The most probable explanation of the absence of any such mention is that Milton's view of the Father and the Son changed after Jeremie Picard had made his fair copy of the treatise.

One other change in the treatise is most conveniently explained by the hypothesis that the anti-Trinitarian view was argued in revisions of and additions to Jeremie Picard's version. In chapter xvii, 'Of Renovation', Milton defines the calling of man in these terms:

> Vocatio est naturalis illa renovationis ratio qua Deus Pater ex praestituto ipsius in Christo, ad agnitionem numinis placandi et colendi, lapsos homines invitat, et credentes quidem ex gratuita benignitate ad salutem non credentes ad tollendam omnem eorum excusationem.

> The calling of man is that natural mode of renovation whereby God the Father, according to his purpose in Christ, invites fallen man to a knowledge of the way in which he is to be propitiated and worshipped; insomuch that believers, through his gratuitous kindness, are called to salvation, and such as refuse to believe are left without excuse. (xv. 344–5.)

The words—' ex praestituto ipsius '—have been added in a later hand, so that Milton had first written simply—' Deus Pater in Christo', etc. This surely can only be interpreted as showing a development in Milton's view towards that separation of the Son from the Father which marked his later belief. 'God the Father in Christ', etc., is a Trinitarian expression, very different from 'God the Father according to his purpose in Christ'.

One other addition to the manuscript seems to

stress the inferiority of the Son in the light of Milton's later thought. In his discussion of the exaltation of Christ by the Father, he has added these words:

> hinc Ioan ii. 19: *destruite templum hoc, et intra triduum excitabo illud.* nempe quia hoc mandatum acceperat a patre, ut ex loco proxime citato fassus est.

> Hence John ii. 19: 'destroy this temple, and in three days I will raise it up', namely, because he had been so commanded by the Father, as he acknowledges in the preceding quotation. (xv. 310–11.)

So far as I can discover, these are the only passages in *De Doctrina Christiana*, after the first fourteen chapters, in which Milton's anti-Trinitarian doctrine is either plainly stated or suggested. If he had reached this view when the work was prepared by Jeremie Picard, we should surely have found some mention of it in these chapters. There was plenty of opportunity for such mention. There were many occasions on which Milton could have found reason to relate his doctrine to the anti-Trinitarian view. When, for example, he quotes 1 Cor. xv. 24–28 with the final words—'that God may be all in all', we should have expected him to remind us of this evidence that the Son is to be subject to the Father. This passage is twice quoted, in chapter xv and chapter xxxiii, but in neither case does Milton even hint the fact that he has already, in chapter v, used it to prove that the Son is inferior to God.

I cannot resist the conclusion that the anti-Trinitarian belief is, on the whole, foreign to the

doctrine set down in the hand of Jeremie Picard.
If we are right in supposing that Jeremie Picard
worked with Milton on the treatise at least as late
as 1659–60, it must follow that the early parts of it
were revised and radically altered after the first two
or three books of *Paradise Lost* were composed.
The study of the doctrine in *Paradise Lost* will, I
think, confirm this view.

Certainly in one point the treatise is at variance
with the poem. In Book III, the Son speaks of his
death in these words:

> Though now to Death I yield, and am his due
> *All that of me can die*, yet that debt paid,
> Thou wilt not leave me in the loathsom grave
> His prey, nor suffer my unspotted Soule
> For ever with corruption there to dwell. (iii. 245 ff.)

In the treatise, Milton discusses the question
whether Christ died in both his natures, human and
divine. So far as his human nature is concerned, he
quickly came to the conclusion that Christ's soul
must have died on the same day as his body.
Whether he yielded to death in his divine nature
was a problem less easy of solution, and Milton had
'greater hesitation' in deciding it. The treatise
shows, first of all, precisely that state of mind
indicated in the words of the poem—'All of me that
can die '. The matter is still doubtful. But a number
of additions to the passage make it clear that Milton
in the end made up his mind. With certain illustra-
tive passages from the Bible, he added these
unequivocal words:

> totus igitur Christus, agnus ille mactatus fuit.

> Christ, therefore, the sacrificial lamb, was slain in the whole of his nature. (xv. 308–9.)

In this point, then, at least, the treatise clearly shows a development forward from the opinion indicated in the poem.

VI

Two marginal additions to the manuscript of *De Doctrina Christiana* seem to come, not from any development in Milton's thought, but from the courage and endurance which were born in him from much suffering and many disappointments. To his discussion of chastisement as an instrument by which God induces repentance in man, he has added these words:

> God however assigns a limit to chastisement, lest we should be overwhelmed, and supplies strength for our support even under those afflictions which, as is sometimes the case, appear to us too heavy to be borne. (xv. 389.)

At the end of the same chapter, Milton finds consolation for those who are sorely afflicted:

> Hence arises consolation to the afflicted. 2 Cor. i. 4: 'who comforteth us in all our tribulation, that we may be able to comfort them that are in any trouble by the comfort wherewith we ourselves are comforted of God'. 1 Thess. iii. 3: 'that no man should be moved by these afflictions; for yourselves know that we are appointed thereunto'. 2 Tim. ii. 3: 'thou therefore endure hardness, as a good soldier of Jesus Christ'. Rev. ii. 9: 'I know thy works and tribulations'. (xv. 391.)

These surely were passages from Scripture with which Milton consoled himself in his own time of tribulation. I cannot help thinking that they must have been written some time after the Restoration.

VII

The most important conclusion we must reach after an examination of *De Doctrina Christiana* and the manuscript in which it is written is this: that we must not too uncritically assume that it may be used as a comment on, and an interpretation of, the doctrinal basis of *Paradise Lost*. We know that Milton's views changed. They may well have changed after the poem was written or during the years of composition. The record of these changes is to be found in the treatise, and it is possible that in it are to be found views and beliefs formulated after Milton had commenced the poem. Only a comparison of the poem with the treatise will help us to decide the relation between them.

In the light of this, we proceed to study the development of Milton's Christian doctrine, bearing in mind the fact that we cannot immediately resolve difficulties in or doubts about any point arising in his works by a simple and straightforward reference to the parallel passages in the treatise. Is *Paradise Lost* anti-Trinitarian? We shall have to answer this question by a method of inquiry different from a simple reference to the chapter, 'Of the Son', in the treatise. What was Milton's true view of free-will and pre-destination? We cannot be sure that when the poem was composed, Milton had framed those

3

weighty arguments to be found in his chapters on God's Decrees. What was Milton's conception of God ? We cannot be sure that the idea of God to be found in the poem is one with the idea of God suggested in the treatise. Did Milton believe that all things are of the substance of God, when he wrote *Paradise Lost* ? The treatise would seem to show that there is no certainty about this, for he certainly once believed that some things were created out of a substance other than God's.

We learn, too, from the treatise certain ideas with which Milton's mind continued to wrestle. It is clear that he was for long puzzled about the nature of Christ, God-Man. He spent much time clearing away the debris that continued to hamper his mind and embarrass his conception of Gospel Liberty. He made sure that men, regenerate and unregenerate, have a certain true freedom of will which makes them responsible if they do not answer God's call. In all the revisions, which the physical state of the manuscript reveals to us, we see a mind vividly at work. From such a mind proceeded *Paradise Lost*.

## II

## AMES AND WOLLEBIUS

### I

MILTON lived in a world busy with ideas: a world in which ideas were not playthings of the mind, but sanctions for the soul. A vivid picture of this world is given by Thomas Edwards, in a pamphlet, *Gangræna*, published in 1646. Edwards writes how the stories of heretics and the reports of heresies were circulated as the familiar gossip of the street-corner and the shop-counter. Heresy was like the plague, and a man would whisper to his neighbour that a common acquaintance had caught it; more, no man could tell from day to day which of his relatives or neighbours would succumb to it.

Edwards quotes a number of cases:

> This *Clement Wrighter* about Spring last did affirm to Mr. *Farthing*, (from whom I have it in writing, written by his own hand) That man hath no immortall Soul, but when he dieth, all of man sleepeth till the Resurrection; and that the Scriptures are not the Word of God. . . .

> On *April* the 9. 1645, being that day commonly called Easter Wednesday, Mr. *Cole* Book-Seller in *Cornhill*, in his own Shop . . . amongst other Discourse told me, That divers persons whom about 4 years ago he thought as godly as any, were now fallen to deny all things in matters of Religion . . . and some of them would come into his Shop, and had spoken fearfull blasphemies not fit to be named; as that the Virgin *Mary* was . . .

(I forbear to mention what followed). . . .

. . . there came in one Mr. *Y*. who related that in his Family there were but four persons, himself, his wife, a man, and a maid-Servant, and saith he, we are of severall Churches and wayes; I am of the Church of *England*, my wife was of one Mr. *Iacies* Church; but she is fallen off from that Church (as many others have) and is now of none, doubting whether there be any Church or no upon the Earth; my Maid-Servant is of *Paul Hobsons*; my man belongs to a company of which there are some twenty or more yong men, who meet together to Exercize, but sing no Psalms. . . .

Edwards made a catalogue in this same pamphlet of 'many of the Errours, Heresies, Blasphemies, and pernicious Passages . . . an extract of many letters all concerning the present sects'. This catalogue is notable because it contains a marginal reference to Milton's views on divorce and also because it mentions many of the heresies to which Milton later subscribed. These are some of the items in the catalogue:

That God hath not decreed all the actions of men, because men doing what God decreed, do not sin.

That God loved not one man more then another before the world, neither is there an absolute particular election, but only general and conditionall on perseverance; and the Scripture no where speaks of Reprobates or Reprobation.

That the soul dies with the body, and all things shall have an end, but God only shall remain for ever.

Every creature in the first estate of creation was God, and every creature is God, every creature that hath life and breath being an efflux from God, and shall returne into God again, be swallowed up in him as a drop is in the ocean.

That Christ died for all men alike, for the reprobate as well as for the elect. . . .

Those Heathen that perish, do perish only for not beleeving according to the Gospel they enjoy.

That regenerate men who have true grace, may fall totally and finally from the state of grace.

That the soul of man is mortall as the soul of a beast, and dies with the body.

That the souls of the faithfull after death, do sleep till the day of judgement, and are not in a capacitie of acting any thing for God, but 'tis with them as 'tis with a man that is in some pleasing dream.

. . . that 'tis as lawfull to baptize a Cat, or a Dog or a Chicken, as to baptize the Infants of beleevers.

That Ministers of the Gospel in these daies ought to work with their hands, and to follow some calling, that they may not be chargeable to the Church.

That 'tis lawfull for a man to put away his wife upon indisposition, unfitnesse or contrariety of minde arising from a cause in nature unchangeable.

(Here is the marginal reference to Milton:)

'Tis lawfull for one man to have two wives at once.

These, then, were some of the heresies which were current in England about 1640, and Milton came later to subscribe to many of them. In 1640, however, he occupied his Sundays in dictating to his nephews, 'some part, from time to time, of a Tractate which he thought fit to collect from the ablest of Divines, who had written on that subject: Amesius, Wollebius, etc.'. Ames and Wollebius were Calvinists and, although they differ both in emphasis and in minor points of doctrine, they were not touched by heretical opinion.

## II

Milton's *De Doctrina Christiana* takes its shape from Ames's *Medulla* and Wollebius's *Compendium*. Like them, it is divided into two books, the first dealing with the Knowledge of God, or Faith, the second with the Worship of God, or Love. Its arrangement into chapters has been borrowed from theirs with certain unimportant modifications arising from Milton's change of view. Like them, it proceeds by way of definition of points of doctrine, illustrated by passages of Scripture, and, where necessary, expanded by argument. Phrases, taken over from these shorter manuals, are still to be found in Milton's treatise, sometimes unaltered, sometimes slightly amended. Edward Phillips spoke truly when he said that the 'Tractate' was originally 'collected' from the work of these two divines.

One example will illustrate the importance that these two works have for us in an understanding of Milton's doctrine. The invocation at the beginning of Book III of *Paradise Lost* has shown itself to be susceptible of several interpretations, and is, indeed, a passage of some difficulty.

> Hail holy Light, ofspring of Heav'n first-born,
> Or of th' Eternal Coeternal beam
> May I express thee unblam'd ? since God is light,
> And never but in unapproached light
> Dwelt from Eternitie, dwelt then in thee,
> Bright effluence of bright essence increate. (iii. 1 ff.)

The question at issue is this: Does Milton here refer to physical light, to the principle of light of which heaven is the very sphere; or does he refer to one, quite properly called 'ofspring of Heav'n first-born', the Son of God, who may well have been held by Milton to be very Light ?

The occasion for the invocation seems to support the view that Milton is addressing physical light. He now returns from Stygian shades to the abode of gods and angels. He welcomes the release from darkness and, indeed, at the close of the previous book, he makes much of the contrast between the kingdom of darkness and the kingdom of light.

If we turn to Wollebius's *Compendium*, we find what I take to be (at least, in part) the source of this invocation. Wollebius is describing the work of the first day of Creation, and he says that it was three-fold—the creation of the angels, the production of the matter of the world, and the emission of light. This is how he speaks of light:

> Lucis primigeniae immissione: quae quidem lux nec ignis elementaris fuit, nec nubes lucida, nec aliud quodpiam corpus, sed qualitas a Deo (qui est lux inaccessa) aeri immissa, postmodum vero quarto die stellis indita. (p. 31.)

There is no need to emphasize the close relation between both thought and wording in Milton and Wollebius. This is further illustrated for us when, in Book VII, Milton speaks of light as a 'radiant cloud' journeying through the 'aery gloom'—thereby taking over from Wollebius the description, 'nubes lucida', which Wollebius himself rejected. No doubt, I think, can remain that in this invocation Milton is addressing, not the Son, but physical light.[1]

Wollebius assists us in still another difficulty. It is clear from *De Doctrina Christiana* that Milton did not always hold the view that all things are made out of the substance of God. It seems, indeed, likely that he once believed that God made the worlds out of a matter which was other than God.[2] *Paradise Lost* seems to me, moreover, to support this view of the development of Milton's thought. We find perhaps an outline of what Milton earlier believed in Wollebius's *Compendium*. In his account of Creation, Wollebius declares that creation was partly 'ex nihilo', partly 'ex materia naturaliter inhabili' (p. 29). This agrees with that statement in Milton's treatise, where he seems to differentiate between the 'substance of God', out of which the Son was generated, and the 'dust of the earth', out of which Adam was formed. In the last chapter of Book I, Wollebius considers whether the world shall be destroyed in its whole substance or shall undergo a complete transformation according to its qualities. In *De Doctrina Christiana* Milton mentions the same problem in order to dismiss it as unimportant. (xvi. 369.) If we remember what Milton plainly says of the nature of causation in his *Artis Logicae plenior Institutio*— namely, that the causes of a thing are *a qua*, *ex qua*, *per quam*, and *propter quam*—I think we must hold it probable that he once agreed with Wollebius.

Ames's *Medulla* was, perhaps, more congenial to

---

[1] I have changed my view on the interpretation of these lines. See my article, 'Milton's *De Doctrina Christiana*,' *Essays and Studies*, 1933, p. 50.    [2] See p. 14 ff.

Milton than Wollebius's *Compendium*. Ames's way of thought was, indeed, much akin to Milton's, as may be seen in a comparison of Ames's *English Puritanism* (1641) with Milton's *Of Reformation touching Church-Discipline in England* (1641). They use much the same arguments in their protests against prelacy. Both have the same simple ideal of the Christian Church, where the pastors are the teachers, chosen by the flock. In Ames's *Medulla*, too, Milton seems to have found much that served him as a guide when he came to write *Paradise Lost*. His story of the Temptation seems to have been modelled on the account Ames gives in his manual,[1] and there is a very close parallel between Milton's description of the consequences of the Fall in *Paradise Lost* and Ames's in his *Medulla*. I find, too, similarities in the two accounts of Creation; certainly, Milton's account in Book VII of the poem is nearer to Ames than to his own chapter on Creation in *De Doctrina Christiana*. More important, however, than these correspondences are certain ideas, suggested by Ames, which seem to have been starting-points for Milton's later belief.

Ames, a strict Puritan, boldly states [2] the view on which Milton everywhere insists, that Adam fell entirely of his own free-will. He says of Adam:

> The principall cause [of the Fall] was man himselfe, by the abuse of his free-will. (p. 57.)

[1] See my article, 'Milton's *De Doctrina Christiana*', *Essays and Studies*, 1933.

[2] My references are to Ames's own translation, *The Marrow of Sacred Divinity*, 1642.

> For he had received that righteousnesse and grace by which he might have persisted in obedience if he would. That righteousnesse and grace was not taken from him before he had sinned. . . . (p. 57.)

So Milton:

> . . . ingrate, he had of mee
> All he could have; I made him just and right,
> Sufficient to have stood, though free to fall. (iii. 97 ff.)

Nevertheless, Ames continues, God did not give to Adam that special grace which would afford him complete protection against the devil's wiles:

> although that strengthning and confirming grace by which the act of sinning should have been actually hindered, and the contrary act of obedience brought forth was not granted unto him, and that by the certaine, wise and just counsell of God. God therefore was in no wise the cause of his *Fall*: neither did he lay upon man a necessity of falling, but man of his own accord, did freely *Fall* from God. (p. 57.)

Milton makes use of the same idea in similar words:

> Omniscient, who in all things wise and just,
> Hinder'd not *Satan* to attempt the minde
> Of Man. (x. 7 ff.)

Milton and Ames were agreed in this, therefore: Adam had both knowledge and power not to disobey, although God hindered not Satan in his attempt on the obedience of man.

There is, too, a liberality in Ames's description of the nature of Faith which must have appealed to Milton. For Ames, like Milton, believed that Faith is both of the intellect and the will, that it possesses the whole man and no single faculty more than another. Faith is for Ames an act of the 'whole man', an act of 'choice', not merely of the intellect, but of man in all his faculties, will and mind joined and penetrated by a goodness, which through faith has become 'our own'.[1] This is, of course, Milton's view.

Finally, Milton found in Ames's *Medulla* the idea which became central in his view of the process by which man may finally become one with God. Raphael's speech to Adam in Book V, lines 469 et seq. of *Paradise Lost* is the clearest statement in Milton's works of that 'scale of perfection' which reaches down from God to his creatures—the scale, by which his creatures may ascend to him again. This is the key to Milton's view of the process of things in time in their relation to God:

O *Adam*, one Almightie is, from whom
All things proceed, and up to him return,
If not deprav'd from good, created all
Such to perfection, one first matter all,
Indu'd with various forms, various degrees
Of substance, and in things that live, of life;
But more refin'd, more spiritous, and pure,
As neerer to him plac't or nearer tending
Each in thir several active Sphears assignd,
Till body up to spirit work, in bounds
Proportiond to each kind. (v. 469 ff.)

[1] See chapters xxvi–xxviii of the *Medulla*.

In this passage Milton seems to have re-interpreted Ames's description of created things in the *Medulla*. Ames explains that all created things are created good, although liable to 'change and corruption'. He declares, too, that none of them is evil, 'to such perfection were they made'. Moreover, in his view all things tend towards God from whom they proceed.

> Goodnesse of a thing created is that perfection whereby it is fit to the use it serves for: Now that use is particular, or universall.
> The Particular is that proper operation to which any thing serves in its proper nature.
> Universal use, is the ordaining of one thing with others, for the perfection of the Universe or whole.
> By this goodnesse all created things in their naturall manner tend to God from whom they came. . . .
> (pp. 37–8.)

From this position, as it is stated in Ames, Milton seems to have developed the more elaborate, but not very different, view of creation found in Raphael's speech to Adam.

Much in the development of Milton's doctrine will always be a matter of conjecture. It is not, I think, too fanciful to think of Milton in those early years, as he dictated passages from Ames and Wollebius to his two nephews, enlarging and making more liberal his own Calvinist outlook by giving special emphasis to certain passages in the works of those two divines. God as light for ever unapproached; Adam's prime responsibility in his act of disobedience to God; faith as an attribute of the whole man; the logical view that the world is not created out of nothing but out of inert dust; the procedure of all things from God up to whom they must return—these ideas were specially congenial to him, and they appear with quickened emphasis and altered significance in his later thought.

# CHRISTIAN DOCTRINE IN MILTON'S EARLIER WORKS

## I

MILTON's earlier works seem to show that until 1659 (or thereabouts) he remained orthodox in many of those points of belief in which later he became most strikingly heterodox. There is clear evidence, for example, that he for long held the orthodox view of the Trinity. In his ode, *On the Morning of Christ's Nativity* (1634), he wrote:

> That glorious Form, that Light unnsufferable,
> And that far-beaming blaze of Majesty,
> Wherewith he wont at Heav'n's high Councel-Table,
> To sit the midst of Trinal Unity,
> He laid aside; and here with us to be,
> Forsook the Courts of everlasting Day
> And chose with us a darksom House of mortal Clay.

In 1641, he spoke of Arians as 'no true friends of Christ'; and in the same year, in his essay *Of Prelaticall Episcopacy*, he specifically denounced the doctrine which he later espoused:

> should hee [Tertullian] move us, that goes about to prove an imparity between *God* the Father, and *God* the Sonne, as these words import in his Booke against *Praxeas*. The Father is the whole substance, but the Son a derivation, and portion of the whole, as he himselfe professes because the Father is greater then me. Beleeve

him now for a faithfull relater of tradition, whom you see such an unfaithfull expounder of the Scripture. (iii. 97.)

In *Tetrachordon*, there is still another clear indication that Milton held the Trinitarian view:

When therefore we would know what right there may be, in ill accidents, to divorce, wee must repaire thither where God professes to teach his servants by the prime institution, and not where we see him intending to dazle sophisters. (iv. 150.)

God who gave the Law is therefore one with Christ of the Gospels.

As late as 1659 or 1660, Milton seems to imply a view of God and the Son of God different at least from that argued in *De Doctrina Christiana*, where the Son is inferior to the Father, of a different essence, and generated in time by God's decree, a creature. In *The Ready and Easie Way to Establish a Free Commonwealth*, he apostrophized the Father and the Son in terms which seem to imply a certain equality:

Thus much I should perhaps have said though I were sure I should have spoken only to trees and stones. . . . Nay though what I have spoke, should happ'n (which Thou suffer not, who didst create mankinde free; nor Thou next, who didst redeem us from being servants of men!) to be the last words of our expiring libertie. (vi. 148.)

And in *A Treatise of Civil Power in Ecclesiastical Causes*, he suggests still more unambiguously a view certainly nearer to the Trinitarian view than his later opinion:

> if bought and by him redeemd who is God from what was once the service of God, we shall be enthrald again and forc'd by men to what now is but the service of men. (vi. 30.)

I cannot believe that Milton would have written like this had he framed the arguments of Chapter V, 'Of the Son', in *De Doctrina Christiana*. If he had already held the anti-Trinitarian view, he would not have weakened his statement and he would have reported his own opinion more faithfully by saying:

> if bought and by him redeemed who is the *Son of God*, etc.

Milton never speaks of the Son as God in *De Doctrina Christiana*—as *deus*, indeed, but not as *Deus*.

It seems probable, then, that Milton held something akin to the Trinitarian view as late as 1659.

Only one passage in Milton's prose works (earlier than 1660) reveals Milton's views of Predestination and God's decrees. In *The Doctrine and Discipline of Divorce*, Book II (1643), he tried to show that God could not permit divorce under the Mosaic Law, if divorce is indeed evil and sinful. To hold such a view would be to make God the author of sin. This leads Milton to consider the nature of God's will and the charges which the 'Jesuits and that sect among us which is named of Arminius are wont' to make 'against us'—and by 'us', Milton clearly means the strict Puritans.

He denies that God has two wills; and in this he takes an orthodox view. We find Wollebius, for example, a strict believer in Predestination in the Calvinist sense, writing: 'The wills of God are not two, or more, or contrary'. But he adds this comment: 'Nevertheless there are various distinctions within the will of God, as the doctrine concerning the decrees, expounded below, will show; but these distinctions are rather in name than in being'.[1] So Milton admits that God's will is twofold:

> The hidden wayes of his providence we adore & search not; but the law is his reveled wil, his complete, his evident, and certain will. (iii. 440.)

His complete, revealed will, that is to say, so far as it concerns us to know. For later in the same chapter, Milton further indicates that God's will is twofold, hidden and revealed:

> 'Tis wonder'd how there can be in God a secret, and reveal'd will; and yet what wonder, if there be in man two answerable causes. But here there must be two revealed wills grappling in a fraternall warre with one another without any reasonable cause apprehended. (iii. 443.)

God's will is, then, twofold, and there are two 'answerable causes' in man. What are they? Surely, first, man's own propensity to sin; and secondly, that divine necessity, working on man, by which God has predetermined all things. This

[1] Op. cit., p. 13.

distinction Milton would later in his life have termed 'scholastic', and he would have found in it a terrible charge against Deity. In *De Doctrina Christiana*, indeed, he has come to the conclusion that to attribute to God a 'twofold' will is 'much the same as to attribute [to him] two distinct wills, whereof one is in direct contradiction to the other'.

A more difficult problem is raised when we consider what Milton has to say about God's decree of Predestination. These are his words:

> Yet considering the perfection wherin man was created, and might have stood, no decree necessitating his free will, but subsequent though not in time yet in order to causes which were in his own power, they might, methinks be perswaded to absolve both God and us. (iii. 441.)

In other words, if the Jesuits and the Arminians will consider the proper nature of Predestination, they might be persuaded to absolve God from responsibility for sin and us from charging him with that. The passage is perplexing, as all the attempts to reconcile God's predestinating decree with the culpability of man are perplexing. Two points are, however, clear. First, man was created perfect and fell of his own choice, no decree necessitating his Fall. In this Milton is in agreement with Ames, who was (and who regarded himself as) one of the 'stricter sort of Puritans'. Secondly, the decree of predestination is subsequent, not in order of time, but in order of causes *which were in man's own power*. The inference is that at this time Milton

believed that there were causes other than those
which lay within the power of man; that is, causes to
be found within God's secret will, in the 'hidden
ways of his providence'. In his later view, a cause is a
cause and necessity is necessity. There could be no
question, when Milton compiled his treatise, of the
causes which were in man's own power and causes
which are to be found elsewhere. Man is wholly and
solely responsible for his fall, and God's decree is not
only subsequent but conditional. *De Doctrina
Christiana* even allows that the decree is subsequent
in order of time to God's foreknowledge of man's
abuse of his free-will—'if we must apply to God a
phraseology borrowed from our own habits and
understanding'. (xiv. 81.)

Although I consider that this reference to God's
will and Predestination in *The Doctrine and Discipline
of Divorce* is not to be interpreted as a departure
from the Calvinist view, I believe that it reveals
something of that 'quarrel with himself' which was
later to disturb and transform Milton's Christian
opinion. There is a certain uneasiness in it. There
is, too, an emphasis on the forthrightness of God and
on the responsibility of man which anticipates the
change of view. We should remember, however, in
all discussion of Milton's attitude to the Calvinist
doctrine of Predestination, that even as late as 1673
he confessed that this doctrine is affirmed 'not
without plea of scripture'. (vi. 169.)

Milton's view of Christian Liberty is bound up
with his opinion relating to the Mosaic Law. There
is clear evidence in the manuscript of *De Doctrina
Christiana* that Milton progressively weakened the

force and the scope of the Mosaic Law. It was for
the Israelites alone. It was utterly abrogated with
the coming of Christ. It could not promise eternal
life, although Jews even before the Gospel could
attain salvation by faith in God. In his early prose
works Milton quotes the Mosaic Law as being still
obligatory on Christian believers and, so far as the
civil law was concerned, in no way abrogated by
Christ.

In the Divorce pamphlets, his line of argument
made it convenient for him to hold that the Mosaic
Law was still in force. The Law is more lenient in
its attitude to divorce than Christ's plain words:
'What therefore God hath joined together, let no
man put asunder'. The Law could be quoted
plainly: Milton had to use a certain adroitness in
argument to dispose of Christ's injunction. Since
the Mosaic Law made divorce (under certain
circumstances) permissible, it was to the advantage
of Milton's argument for him to say of God:

> The vigor of his Law could no more remit, then the
> hallowed fire on his altar could be let goe out. The
> Lamps that burnt before him might need snuffing, but
> the light of his Law never. (iii. 440.)

It is unnecessary to quote the many passages in
the Divorce pamphlets in which Milton speaks of
'the divine law, which Christ did not abolish'. All
of them point to the fact that his view of Gospel
Liberty, his idea of the relation between works and
faith, could not have attained that rational simplicity
which marks his description of these things in *De
Doctrina Christiana*.

In 1659 Milton's view of the Law was changing, and he throws grave doubt on these earlier statements in a passage in *A Treatise of Civil Power in Ecclesiastical Causes*:

> As for civil crimes and of the outward man, which all are not, no not of those against the second table, as that of coveting; in them what power they have, they had from the beginning, long before *Moses* or the two tables were in being. And whether they be not now as little in being to be kept by any Christian as they are two legal tables, remanes as yet undecided, as it is sure they never were yet deliverd to the keeping of any Christian magistrate. But of these things perhaps more some other time. (vi. 40.)

In this treatise, therefore, for the first time Milton begins to speak vigorously of that sweeping away of the 'weak and beggarly rudiments' of the Law, which until the Gospel had served instead of man's free conscience. He does not yet say that the whole of the Mosaic Law was abrogated; but his mind is reaching forward to that position. His perception of Christian liberty grows clearer and more unhampered:

> Hence it planely appears, that if we be not free we are not sons, but still servants unadopted; and if we turn again to those weak and beggarly rudiments, we are not free; yea though willingly and with a misguided conscience we desire to be in bondage to them. (vi. 31.)

The whole of the Mosaic Law was in great danger of being abrogated when Milton could write like this.

The early prose works help us to an understanding

of Milton's view of definite points of doctrine only
by implication and in incidental references. There is
a clear point of change in Milton's attitude to the
Law, but apart from that there is no evidence of any
shift of opinion. Before 1650, there is clear evidence
that Milton was a Trinitarian; after 1650, he writes
of the Father and the Son in a manner to which no
Trinitarian could object and which is not easily
reconciled with his later views. Certainly before
1650 he accepted the Calvinist view of God's
decrees and Predestination. How far he concealed
a change of view, how long his orthodoxy really
lasted, we cannot tell. On these points, his early
prose works can tell us little. All we can say is that
they give no clear evidence of a change of view
except, in 1659, in Milton's attitude to the Mosaic
Law.

Milton is not concerned with a system of Christian
doctrine in these earlier prose works: he is concerned
with particular controversies. His manner of carry-
ing on these controversies, the opinions he supports,
the arguments he uses may tell us something of the
mood and the mind which, after all, precedes and
determines any change in belief. These reveal something of his view of God, something of his view of
liberty—the affection of his whole spirit, not only the
reasoning of his intellect. And out of affection or
disaffection must have arisen his change of opinion.

## II

*De Doctrina Christiana* and *Paradise Lost* report a
mind searching, not altogether easily, for some way

of reconciliation between God and man. They are the work of a man whose spirit has been unsettled in his faith in God and his trust in man. They are Milton's attempt to settle a certain quarrel with himself—and the terms of that quarrel are not simple but many. The nature of God plays a large part in it. How can he be omnipotent and we be free ? How can he be good and we be evil ? Milton is restless in the presence of God, partly because of the conflicting awarenesses of God's nature in his own mind, partly because of his abundant consciousness of man's freedom, man's responsibility, and man's depravity. To make his peace with God —this aim lies behind the argument of *De Doctrina Christiana*: it is the very agony and sincerity of *Paradise Lost*.

Agony and, I think, even sincerity (of this kind) are absent from the earlier prose works. As we read them, we have the feeling that the nature of God is largely taken for granted, and that Milton is chiefly concerned to defend against merely human assaults that freedom which he instinctively prized. He writes of God as though his faith in God had not been disturbed, as though the subscription of his mind had never been shaken by the deeper perplexities of his heart. He writes of a freedom which is either political or psychological; of a will which is the slave of prelate or potentate or passion—not of spiritual freedom, not of a will enfranchised by faith. His belief in God had not been proved by disillusionment or moody questioning. He understands freedom chiefly in terms of the attacks that may be made on it from within and from without—he is able to accept without criticism that service which became for him perfect freedom.

There is no doubt that he thought of himself as specially favoured of God. He had that 'egotistical sublime' in his temper which made him regard himself as the special servant of the Almighty. He seems not so much to have given himself up to the guidance of the Holy Spirit as to have been continually confirmed in his expectation that the Holy Spirit's promptings would exactly agree with his own. He was confident—what reason had he to question it?—that the Almighty was on his side in the battle of life, in the battle of wits, in contemporary strife. He did not expect that that side would be the losing side. He is not diffident before God in these early works. There seems to have been no occasion for him to turn the searchlight of self-criticism on his conception of God in these early years. His belief had not yet been shaken.

In the Divorce pamphlets, God appears chiefly as the giver of a law of which Milton could heartily approve. As we read these pamphlets, we are not convinced that the nature of God nor even Milton's view of God has very much to do with the development of the argument. Milton calls upon the authority of God, not his nature. What energy of persuasion these writings have derives chiefly from Milton's own passionate understanding of domestic freedom, not from any vision of what is just and pleasing in the sight of God. It is true that he ventures on certain descriptions of God. God is 'pure spirit'; the Law is the 'perfect rule of his own purest will'; 'God sends remedies as well as evils';

'God prefers the free and cheerful worship of a Christian'; 'God delights not'—nor, indeed, does Milton in this connexion—'to make a drudge of virtue, whose actions must be all elective and unconstrained'. On the whole, however, there is a certain *innocence* in Milton's references to God. He is—if one may use the expression—a little free with his name.

The pamphlets written in defence of people and church against prelate and king before the Commonwealth and in its early years show, too, that while Milton could deal doughty blows in what he conceived to be the cause of God, he assumed perhaps a little too easily that his cause was indeed God's cause. It is true that there is in these works a consciousness of that perfect worship of God which marks the fine Protestant individualism of Milton's day. This consciousness, however, does not seem in Milton to be grounded in a simple, integral, and weathered faith. There are 'adjuvant causes' working in his belief and faith. These were his conviction that God had a special charge for him and a special care and mission for his country.

Milton very often speaks as though God had chosen him for special work. It is certain that in his ambition to write a great poem, to 'leave something so written to aftertimes, as they should not willingly let die', he believed himself to be marked out by God. He is to do for England what the great poets have done for the Hebrews and the Greeks. To perform such work needed abilities 'not in their divine argument alone, but in the very critical act of composition'.

'These abilities', he says, 'wheresoever they be found, are
the inspired guift of God rarely bestow'd, but yet to
some (though most abuse) in every Nation'. (iii. 238.)

What kind of a poem does he propose to write ?
Surely a poem very different from *Paradise Lost*:
not one that would 'justify God's ways with men',
but one that would 'celebrate' and 'glorify' God's
name. He means to 'celebrate in glorious and lofty'
hymns 'the throne and equipage of God's almighti-
ness, and what he works, and what he suffers to be
wrought with high providence in his church', and
'to deplore the general relapses of kingdoms and
states from justice and God's true worship'.
(iii. 238.)

A large number of subjects presented themselves
to him, and of these two seem to have been chiefly
considered: King Arthur and his Knights, mentioned in *Epitaphium Damoniis*; Paradise Lost and
the Fall of Man, sketched as a tragedy in four
different drafts in the Milton MSS. preserved in
Trinity College, Cambridge.

Milton seems to have had the first of these two
subjects in mind when he speaks, in *The Reason of
Church Government*, of a poem which shall teach
'over the whole book of sanctity and vertu through
all the instances of example with such delight to
those especially of soft and delicious temper who
will not so much as look upon Truth herself, unlesse
they see her elegantly dresst'. (iii. 239.) For who
can doubt that he had Spenser in mind as he wrote
those words ? There is, indeed, in the project a kind
of imitativeness, a borrowed inspiration, which

supports the view that Milton had not yet known that deep experience of God, which includes doubt, and which alone could give energy and authenticity to his poem. He has not as yet those resources of experience which would enable him to write a great poem wholly his own.

The projects for a tragedy do not introduce the person of God or, indeed, any of the persons of the Trinity. They tell us nothing of Milton's view of God, although they indicate that he was very early in his life interested in the Fall of men and angels as a subject for poetical treatment. The drafts *might* have been written in the same mood in which *Paradise Lost* was written: the evidence they provide of mood is too sparse for any judgement to be made on it. They read to me, however, like the writing of a man who has set his hand to a work he deems great: they are the foundations of a building whose form and finish are not in doubt.

Not even Milton's blindness disturbed his view that God had a special care for him. In *The Second Defence of the People of England*, he not only declared that he had 'examined himself' without finding 'any offense', which might deservedly have 'called down this calamity' upon him; he also claims that he enjoys in no small degree the favour of the Deity, who regarded him 'with greater clemency and benignity' in proportion as he was able to behold nothing but God himself. (viii. 67–71.) God, he believed, was wont to illuminate him with 'an inward and far surpassing light'. God had, indeed, specially enlarged his faculties, had veritably chosen him and equipped him for the work of writing these defences. He is, he says, 'under the care of the Deity' and, 'though in no wise free from the ills of humanity', he is 'aided by the divine favour and help'. (viii. 19.)

God had also, as Milton believed, a special care for England. Milton's patriotism is always expressed in terms of God's special providence. The English people, he thought, had been chosen by God to lead the world in liberty and true religion. They had fallen off, indeed, since the Almighty had shown in Wycliffe his special purpose for them; but now, in Milton's time, there was opportunity enough for them to fulfil that purpose. Naturally Milton had the assured feeling that God was on the side of the Parliament and that Cromwell was in a special sense his chosen instrument. In his *Defence of the People of England*, he asked:

> Yet why do I proclaim as done by the people these actions, which themselves almost utter a voice, and witness everywhere the presence of God ? (vii. 5.)

And, in his conclusion, he writes to the people of England:

> Gloriously hath he [God] delivered you before all other nations from what surely are the two greatest mischiefs of this life, and most pernicious to virtue—Tyranny and Superstition; he hath inspired you with the greatness of soul to be the first of mankind. . . . (vii. 553.)

In *The Second Defence*, this belief in the special providence of God is focused on Cromwell:

For, while you, O Cromwell, are in safety, he shows not
a sufficient confidence in the supreme, who has any fears
for the prosperity of England; seeing, as he must, that
God so manifestly favours you, that, in all things he is
your helper. (viii. 219.)

That 'confidence in the Supreme', though not
destroyed, must have been gravely challenged, when
even Cromwell came to be doubted.

In the political works, written just before the
Restoration, there is a change in Milton's mood. In
his letter concerning *The Ruptures of the Commonwealth*, the old confidence is gone. Cromwell is dead
and the people were clamouring for the Restoration. Milton's mood becomes one of shame and
humiliation, and he speaks of God in another tone.
Now he fears that the heavy judgement of God, 'who
cannot but avenge these hypocrisies, violations of truth
and holiness', may come down upon the English
people. And at the close of *The Ready and Easie Way
to Establish a Free Commonwealth* (1660), he addresses
God with a humility, with a depth of suppliant
feeling, almost strange and foreign to his earlier
work. There is despair and little hope for the
future in his words. The people have departed from
God and 'choose them a captain back from Egypt'.
Milton does not now warn them of the heavy
judgement; he does not admonish them and call upon
them to fulfil the high mission with which God had
charged them. He turns to God as an appellant—
how rarely he has done this before!—and pleads
that God prevent the end that he fears for his
country:

which Thou suffer not, who didst create man free; nor
Thou next, who didst redeem us from being servants
of men!

Here is a change indeed. England had forsaken
God, and Milton's belief in God had to find ground
more assured than the high mission and triumph of
his native country. More, he himself must have felt
alone and chastened; his own mission was called in
question. Is it not probable that now he was left
with a conception of God which suddenly appeared
as a 'bundle of impossibles and inconceivables';
with the Calvinist conception of God without that
high social optimism which made such a conception
tolerable and reasonable? Is it not probable that
now Milton would begin to feel that his Christian
doctrine needed to be 're-formed' 'after a more
accurate model'?

### III

The constant theme of Milton's prose works
before 1660 is the theme of liberty. It would be
easy to make a gibe at Milton's passion for liberty
and to point out that the liberty he seems chiefly to
have desired was liberty for himself. It is easy—too
easy, indeed—to suggest that a 'mute and spiritless
mate' was the occasion for the Divorce pamphlets:
that a doubt as to whether his own work would pass
the licenser was the occasion for *Areopagitica*. It is
easy, on the other hand, to point out that Milton
pleaded for liberty when there was no advantage to
him in doing so, when it seemed that his fellow-

countrymen set no such value on liberty as he desired. There is a courageous consistency in Milton's views that bids us dismiss the sneers to which he laid himself open as mean-spirited misunderstandings of a mind, too honest to doubt even its own integrity. Milton did believe in liberty; and invasions of his own liberty prompted him to discover where most true liberty is threatened. His vision of liberty is none the less wise and noble because his own was once impaired; wiser and nobler, indeed, when in those later years he was left solitary and nothing was left for him to defend liberty or to give it sanction except the vigour of his intellect and the independence of his spirit.

What kind of a liberty is it that Milton pleads for in these earlier works ?

He is not—such was the depravity of man, he never was—an anarchist. It is true, he says, that 'all men naturally were born free, being the image and resemblance of God himself'. But, with the fall of Adam, they do 'wrong and violence' and, in consequence, agreed to bind themselves in a 'mutual league' as defence against such as do them injury. For Milton, the best government was certainly self-government, whether political or psychological. But such as would not and could not govern themselves are better governed by others. We are left in no doubt as to whom these are who are incapable of governing themselves; likewise, we are left in no doubt as to whom are worthy of liberty.

I confess there are but few, [Milton wrote] and those men of great wisdom and courage, that are either

desirous of liberty or capable of using it.  Far the
greatest part of the world prefers just masters.  (vii. 75.)

It is not difficult to discover where Milton would
look for 'these few' amongst the men of his own
time.  It is for these chiefly that he claims freedom
from monarch and bishop.  Not with the peers will
such men be found—for of the peers, there 'may not
be one man deserving the appellation' of 'optimes'.
Nor will they be found amongst the common people,
who are 'blind and brutish'.  These sections of the
nation are diverted 'either by luxury or plenty, or by
want and poverty, from virtue, and the study of
laws and government'.  When Milton writes of
political liberty, he is thinking of the 'middle sort'—
amongst whom are generally found 'the most
prudent men, and most skilful in affairs' (vii. 398).
These are the men who should be free to govern
themselves—and others.

As the years of the Commonwealth passed and
Milton was more and more disappointed by the
conduct and policies even of the 'middle sort', and as
later he heard around him the clamour of enthusiasm
for the Restoration, Milton was put to strange shifts
to invent a state in which liberty should be preserved.  He came to propose, for example, a 'perpetual oligarchy' whose business it would be
(strange means for such an end!) to protect liberty
of conscience and the rights of man.  He saw freedom
now in settlement, in firm and continuous government by a permanent council of just men.  He, who
had seen so many commotions and novelties and had
welcomed them as good, came to object to 'transi-

tory' parliaments, in that they were 'much likelier to unsettle, rather than to settle, a free government, to breed commotions, novelties, and uncertainties'.

His view of liberty had not changed: he only thought that fewer men were worthy of it and that many perils more nearly beset it. He is indeed indifferent to political liberty except in so far as it means liberty for the virtuous man. The free man is the virtuous man and 'none can love freedom heartily but good men'. But he saw a people 'basely and besottedly' ready 'to run their necks again into the yoke'. He concludes that liberty is not for them.

His view of liberty and his pleas for it are grounded in his trust of the 'middle sort'. Most appeals for freedom are based in a confident belief in the goodness of human nature—or, just as often, in a belief that men will at least pursue their own true advantage. The moral justification for political freedom is the right of each man to develop without restraint his own personality. Milton never had much faith in the generality of men and he knew of no right that men (other than the 'regenerate') might have to develop their personalities except within closely-prescribed lines. Those lines were prescribed by the class to which Milton belonged and for whom he wrote—the 'middle sort'. In all his political works, written in the early years of the Commonwealth, he shows his contempt both for the peers and the rabble. He denounces the sensuality and licence of the court; he pours a hearty bourgeois contempt on serving-men and mean mechanics.

He was never a leveller: only circumstances made him a revolutionary.

Freedom is indeed rooted for him at this time in the practical morality of his class. Its high value is one with strenuous and sturdy Protestant individualism. Thrift and the conquest of sensuality and the avoidance of all luxury are its manifestations and its guarantees:

> Unless you banish avarice, ambition, luxury from your thoughts, and all excess even from your families, the tyrant, whom you imagined was to be sought abroad, and in the field, you will find at home, you will find within, and that a more inexorable one. (viii. 241.)

When Milton began to see around him the signs of this other tyranny, he grew melancholy for the state of the country and devised strange plans in his fancy to conserve what freedom—that is, what avoidance of luxury, what strict living—remained. He proposed a 'permanent council' and a severely restricted franchise—as though the tyranny without is not so dangerous as the tyranny within. These are the schemes of a despairing man. Milton knows what are the conditions of freedom in the virtuous man; but he knows, too, that men do not naturally seek it. What kind of civil government will most surely make it possible ? One in which 'they who are the greatest, are perpetual servants and drudges to the public at their own cost and charges, neglect their own affairs, yet are not elevated above their brethren'. He has little hope that such will be the state of things in the England of his time. Where, then, shall those who are worthy and desirous of freedom find it ? On whom must men rely for freedom if they cannot rely on themselves ? Milton is prompted by the turn of social events to look for a supernatural sanction for freedom in the nature of Grace, in God.

## IV

In precisely the same way, Milton's view of religious liberty—that freedom in belief and opinion which the Christian has the right to demand of the civil magistracy—was a limited view. There are restrictions on the adventures of the mind which Milton would allow to the searcher after religious truth; those restrictions are defined by the Scriptures. He bases his view on the central maxim of Protestantism: 'No man can judge definitely the sense of scripture to another man's conscience'. The authority of the Bible is substituted for the authority of the Church; and religious liberty must begin with an acceptance of the sole authority of the Bible. Milton always hedges in his view of religious liberty with the words: I mean not papists.

*Areopagitica* is justly regarded as the great English prose testimonial of liberty. This it is, but in our admiration for the noble argument, we should not forget that even here Milton pleads for liberty chiefly for himself and his own sort. And he would limit this liberty. He denounces licensing; but he admits that 'it is of greatest concernment in the church and commonwealth, to have a vigilant eye how books demean themselves, as well as men'. He denies not that it may be necessary to 'confine, imprison, and do sharpest judgement on them as malefactors'. In his plea for books, he admits not 'tolerated popery, and open superstition', nor anything 'impious and evil'. If, indeed, any book comes forth which may be considered 'mischievous and libellous', there are timely remedies against it which Milton would use—'the fire and the executioner'.

*Areopagitica* is a Protestant document. Behind it burns that passion for sifting truth from falsehood which was the endeavour of seventeenth-century minds; and Milton speaks persuasively of 'truth', which cannot be put to the worst 'in a free and open encounter'. But this truth, for which man may argue and wrestle, is truth in 'indifferent things'. The fundamentals of the Protestant faith may not be questioned.

Thought frees itself from its confines and often goes farther than it would. There are magnificent passages in Milton's *Areopagitica* which might well be remembered to-day; for they plead for a freedom we tend to under-estimate. But we should remember that in its author's mind it was a plea against licensing; it sets limits to the freedom it would ask for books.

In the anti-prelatical works, Milton clearly states the kind of liberty he is anxious to preserve. The power of the prelate is an infringement of Gospel liberty; it is an impoverishment of that freedom with which Christ's coming endowed all believers.

This is the argument which lies behind all the denunciations of prelacy. The simplicity of the

Reformed faith demands a simplicity of Church government, for it rests on the purity, the uncomplicated austerity of Gospel liberty. We are redeemed from the law of ceremonies by Christ; shall a prelate, then, deny to us the benefits of that redemption ? A simple ministry shall teach and guide us; shall we despoil that simplicity by preserving the superstitious tyranny of priesthood ?

The implications of all these Protestant pleas for religious liberty are clear. As we read them, however, we cannot be sure that Milton has truly related this Gospel Liberty, which is the fundamental element in the Reformed faith, to a conception of God which would most enrich it. Liberty still seems to be for him the absence of restraint on the Christian believer rather than that free and spontaneous bringing forth of good works which he finds in *De Doctrina Christiana* to be the fruits of faith. He still seems to be looking at liberty from the outside and taking its nature for granted. His argument does not proceed from the nature, but from the fact of Gospel Liberty. His readers understand with him what this liberty is all about and he has no need to justify and describe it. The mind in action does not examine and analyse common ground: it only disturbs the ground of debate.

When, however, he begins to argue from the nature of Gospel Liberty, a new reasonableness enters into his work. *A Treatise of Civil Power in Ecclesiastical Causes* (1659) shows how the occasion of controversy could quicken Milton's mind to the examination of his views. In the anti-prelatical

works, he denounced prelacy by a reference to a
Gospel Liberty which he believed his readers to
accept as he accepted it. Here, he argues from the
very nature of that liberty. He describes it and
examines it to prove his point. In the anti-prelatical
works, he seemed to say: How can you accept
prelacy, if you accept—as you do, if you are Protestant—Gospel Liberty ? Now he seems to say:
This is what Gospel Liberty is : how can you tolerate,
then, the interference of the civil magistrates in
spiritual matters ?

In this *Treatise*, there are evidences of a mind
which has debated the problem of liberty with itself.
There are signs that Milton has endeavoured to
clarify for himself the relation between liberty and
law, to make liberty free from all embarrassments.
More, there is an eloquent lucidity in the description
of liberty, unparalleled in the earlier works:

> If then both our beleef and practise, which comprehend
> our whole religion, flow from faculties of the inward
> man, free and unconstrainable of themselves by nature,
> and our practise not only from faculties endu'd with
> freedom, but from love and charitie besides, incapable of
> force, and all these things by transgression lost, but
> renewd and regenerated in us by the power and gift of
> God alone, how can such religion as this admit of force
> by man, or force be any way appli'd to such religion,
> especially under the free offer of grace in the gospel,
> but it must forthwith frustrate and make of no effect
> both the religion and the gospel ? (vi. 21.)

I know of no passage like this in the earlier prose
works; but it is paralleled in *De Doctrina Christiana*.

Consider, too, the temper in which *A Treatise of Civil Power* was written. The old asperity in argument has gone; gone, too, is the old assertive confidence in the citation of scripture. Milton is not less inwardly certain of the rightness of his cause, but modesty implies a quieter confidence. The treatise is written by a man who is satisfied with his argument, even though no notice is taken of his case; by a man who has been more concerned to satisfy himself with the movement of his own thought than to score a victory in the sharpness of debate or to reinforce his cause with spirited propaganda. The earlier Milton is often content to ground his argument in ingenious reference to the Scriptures, in persuasive logic; now he seeks to ground it in the central principles from which it springs.

v

An attentive study of Milton's earlier works must show that he thought of liberty in the individual chiefly at the psychological level. His position seems to have been something like this: Christ has brought us Gospel Liberty, and no shadow should cloud it; this Gospel Liberty is our dearest possession, and with it, we are responsible to God; it consists—and this was where Milton did not yet proceed beyond the psychological inquiry, beyond the abstract and not altogether satisfactory notion of the Reason in control of the passions. Liberty consists—in what? There are many descriptions of it, but none of them grounds liberty in a knowledge of spiritual things, in

Faith, which is 'the very form of good works'. Who can doubt, considering *Comus*, the *Areopagitica*, the Divorce pamphlets, that Milton has been chiefly concerned with infringements of liberty from without and impoverishments of liberty from within ? Nowhere is there adequate mention of the *enrichment*, the enfranchisement of the will from without, from God and the knowledge of God. Milton surely made the examination which was to acquaint him with these when the assaults on liberty and the decay of true liberty in other men were like to leave him comfortless.

*De Doctrina Christiana* shows that Milton's conception of Christian Liberty did indeed move away from the psychological to the spiritual plane. He found at last a supernatural sanction for the freedom of the will. In Chapter XVIII of the treatise, 'Of Regeneration', an addition to the manuscript makes this clear. His first description of regeneration spoke of the destruction of the 'old man', the regeneration of the 'inward man' after the image of God, and the sanctification of the 'whole man, both in body and soul', for the service of God. This did not satisfy him. Milton needed something other than a repetition of the thought of earlier divines. A later thought is recorded in words added to the beginning of the chapter:

> The intent of supernatural Renovation is *not only* to restore man more completely than before to the use of his natural faculties, as regards his power to form right judgement, and to exercize free will; but to create afresh, as it were, the inward man, and *infuse from*

*above new and supernatural faculties into the minds of
the renovated* [my italics]. (xv. 367.)

What do these words imply ? Surely, the words
'not only' suggest that Milton had himself become
aware that he had considered Christian Liberty too
much on the 'natural', the psychological level; and
the concluding sentence shows that in his later
thought he aimed to bring regenerate man into
closer and supernatural touch with God.

The early works bear out this view of the development of Milton's thought in two ways. First, they
show a mind preoccupied with the idea of freedom on
the psychological plane, concerned with the 'natural
man'. Secondly, there are many indications in them
that this view was not wholly satisfying to Milton's
spirit.

The *Areopagitica* speaks of that 'freedom to
choose' and that 'reason which is but choosing' with
which God endowed Adam and all men. It speaks,
too, of a virtue which is only pleasing to God in so
far as it is not a 'cloistered virtue', in so far as it is
sustained and enriched amidst all the invitations to
vice. It makes clear that for Milton true virtue is the
right control of passion by reason. Goodness lies in
a deliberate temperance, a well-judged moderation.
There is little, I think, to differentiate this 'reason'
from that merely 'natural reason' of which Milton
speaks in *De Doctrina Christiana* and which merely
enables men to 'resist bad desires'.

This view of man's freedom persists throughout
the prose works. In the *Second Defence*, Milton
wrote:

Do you, therefore, who have the wish to continue free
. . . learn to obey right reason, to be masters of
yourselves. (viii. 251.)

In the same work he defines freedom in these
terms:

. . . to be free is precisely the same thing as to be pious,
wise, just and temperate, careful of one's own, abstinent
from what is another's, and thence, in fine, mag-
nanimous and brave. (viii. 249.)

Freedom, in the Divorce pamphlets, is conceived by
Milton in terms of his own emotional and psychological experience. He knows that uxoriousness and
a lustful union are breaches of true freedom; but the
worst breach of all is an unsatisfactory mate. He can
give empirical descriptions of freedom in married
life: in the *Doctrine and Discipline of Divorce*, he
speaks of

the ordinance of our solace and contentment, the
remedy of our loneliness.
the apt and cheerful conversation of man with woman,
to comfort and refresh him against the evils of solitary
life.

True, it was not Milton's business to inquire further
into the nature of Christian freedom in these
pamphlets. They give the impression that he
minded his business.

His spirit seems to have been uneasy while his
mind confined itself to an examination of freedom on

this level. Certainly, his 'inward man' was scarcely free in these earlier years. In *Comus* the too brusque opposition of Chastity and Sensual Indulgence comes from a mind hampered by fear of the flesh, made austere by an escape into 'restrictive virtue'. When Milton puts into the mouth of Comus his lavish justification of goodly enjoyments, he writes with enthusiasm—as though he would release a pressure on his spirit. His mind has not yet turned to God for an understanding of true freedom.

The extravagant bitterness of abuse in the controversial works reveals a soul not wholly at ease, not truly free. Why does Milton accuse his enemies of gross sensuality ? Why does he dally so long with the nature of their viciousness ? Why does he jeer at them for their effeminacy, their submission to the rule of their wives, their amorous escapades ? Why does he dwell on petticoats and serving-maids ? This is something more than the contemporary rigours of controversy and the heat of debate; there is an uneasy spirit behind it all.

Milton's view of the free man, in these days, was likely to be empirical, to be determined by his vision of the man he would most like to be—in natural terms. In his descriptions of freedom he makes a portrait of his own 'persona', the man he tried to present both to himself and to the world. Of the nature of Christian Liberty he remained uncritical; he was content to take his description of it from other theologians. Not until he was driven back to make a profound re-examination of his own relation with God; not until his personal problems were more settled; not until freedom in other men, even of the 'middle sort', seemed poor and precarious, would he be prompted to amplify his conception of liberty, to re-fashion and re-discover supernatural sanction for it.

# IV

# CHRISTIAN DOCTRINE IN 'PARADISE LOST'

## I

DURING the latter half of the decade 1650–60, the wind began to go out of Milton's sails. Since the substance of his belief in God had been to a large extent his conviction that God had a special mission for England and for himself; since his habitual way of thinking about God had been in terms of these missions, his view of God was impoverished and starved of significance, when it began to look as though both missions might be nothing more than illusions. Everything that had given him hope from God for so many years was in danger of being utterly cancelled. He was left with a conception of God compelling to his mind but chilling to his heart.

He must have found that he had been resting his belief in God on hope, not on faith. There is an addition to the manuscript of *De Doctrina Christiana* which almost suggests that Milton came to realize the nature of his own problem.

> 'Hope differs from faith', he said, 'as the effect from the cause; it differs from it likewise in its object: for the object of faith is the promise; that of hope, the thing promised'. (xv. 409.)

For a long time Milton's hope had not been

well-grounded in faith: rather had his faith been
sustained too much by hope.

When hope was disappointed, there remained a
view of God that was chiefly a construction of the
mind separate from and unreconciled to the consciousness of God which he felt in his whole being.
The terrible thought of an omnipotent and avenging
Deity must often have possessed him—manfully
faced, moreover, the awful logic of the Calvinist
view of God was not easy to escape. Escape it he
must, for he could not rest content on it. He could
not rest content on a belief that robbed man of his
freedom and—for this followed—of his responsibility. His mind, perhaps without his being com-
pletely aware of it, had moved too far from the
Calvinist view for him to return to it. There was
division, then, and doubt; there was a new 'quarrel
with himself'. *Paradise Lost* is, partly, the record of
this quarrel, partly of the process by which it was
settled.

The consciousness of God remained; but it had
to be transformed and properly reported by the
intellect. What could be the nature of God—now
that Milton could no longer believe in the special
care of God for his people? In what relation could
Milton, could all men stand with God, now that it
seemed no longer possible that God had chosen
Milton and England for a special work? What
were God's ways with men? And how could Milton
himself, in a more private and hidden way, hold
himself responsible before God?

Milton could not utterly renounce the cause of
freedom when that cause seemed lost. Just as his

consciousness of God was transformed, so also was his idea of man's freedom and responsibility. Political freedom seemed vain; the freedom of the natural man was precarious. Who was worthy of political freedom ? How could men's passions—slavish and ready to yield as they had proved—be controlled by reason ? Where should man find virtue ? It is clear, I think, that Milton came to believe that political freedom was nothing and natural freedom a delusion, save for the regenerate man who had been made free by faith.

We can reconstruct a credible picture of Milton's mind about the time of the Restoration. It is not a defeated mind, for it turns bravely and tenaciously to heavy tasks—which doubtless it thought blessed of God. It is not a wholly dispirited mind. There are positive elements in it which must have sustained Milton throughout his later years. Blind as he was and cut off from public affairs, he must have felt himself more than ever alone with God; so much alone that he could write a poem and compile (or revise) a treatise in an endeavour to understand the nature of God and his ways. It was a perplexed mind. Framed in it (and in his 'body of Divinity', so far as it had gone) was a conception of God which was little more than a catalogue of absolutes; and this catalogue was inadequate, serving Milton neither for the past nor for the present as a description of his God. More: this catalogue of absolutes was difficult to reconcile with his belief that men must be both free and responsible. For this belief, too, was positive in his mind. More and more, he had come to discover in Gospel Liberty that coven-

ant which completed man's enfranchisement so that
no shadow of Law or compulsion clouded it.
Though solitary—all the more for being solitary—
he knew himself to be free before God.

This, it seems to me, is the key to Milton's later
poems and to the composition and revision of *De
Doctrina Christiana*. The departures from orthodox
belief in the treatise are best understood as moments
in Milton's intellectual search for a reconciliation
between man and God. These moments brought
Milton closer to a satisfactory system, but many
mysteries remained which he was content not to
probe, and we can read in *Samson Agonistes* the
conclusion that no mere system could settle Milton's
problem for him. *Paradise Lost* is a sublime attempt
to comprehend the whole story of God and man;
but who can deny that Milton was not only embar-
rassed by the needs of his fable, but also by the
intellectual uncertainties and hesitations in his
belief? Out of the embarrassment, indeed, arises
the most moving poetry. Milton was not of the
Devil's party, but no account of the poem is adequate
without some consideration of the reasons which led
Blake to say that he was. We understand *Paradise
Lost* best in terms of the conflict it reports. *Paradise
Regained* aims at something smaller, and it may be
true that Milton was more content with it; for the
modesty of the intention bespeaks a mind already
limiting the scope of its inquiries, already submitting
to what cannot be understood. The main theme of
*Samson Agonistes*, the theme that properly expresses
the mood in which the play was written, is the need
for acceptance and obedience.

The strange thing is that the two poems and the play are only with difficulty brought into relation with the treatise. It cannot be said that the original views, argued so logically and with such detail in *De Doctrina Christiana*, are of central significance in the poem. The very fact that eighteenth-century theologians could find *Paradise Lost ex omne parte orthodoxum* shows at least that the unorthodox elements hardly determine or colour the scheme of the poem. It has been suggested that Milton may have consciously modified his views in writing the poem. If that is so, they cannot have wholly or importantly satisfied the deep needs of his spirit. On any hypothesis we must still say that the mind which compiled *De Doctrina Christiana* and defended with so much energy the unorthodox parts of it was concerned with certain points of doctrine which have no major importance in *Paradise Lost*. These points of doctrine are: the generation of the Son in time pursuant to a decree; the assumption by the Son, not only of human nature, but also of man; the death both of Christ and of men in the whole of their natures; the creation of the world out of the substance of Deity; the reconciliation of man's free-will with God's foreknowledge. Only the last of these plays an important part in the poem, and it is generally admitted that the discussion of free-will and foreknowledge receives unsatisfactory treatment in *Paradise Lost*. Is it not strange? Here we have an intellect which has, whatever view we may accept of the date of *De Doctrina Christiana*, busied itself with the profound mysteries of the Christian religion. We turn to the poems which are the product at least

6

in part of that intellect, and we have to make subtle and unsatisfactory search for evidence of the conclusions of all this intellectual wrestling.

There is one hypothesis which seems to me to take account of these discrepancies. It dovetails, not only with Milton's thoughts and arguments, but also with the development of his mood and temper as these are revealed in the poems. The remaining parts of this study will explore this hypothesis, which I now briefly state.

During the closing years of the Commonwealth, Milton was disturbed into a new questioning of the fundamentals of his faith. The deep certitudes of God and free-will were not questioned: these were secure in the foundations of his being. But his understanding of these certitudes, the arguments by which he defended them, the system into which he framed them—all these came to be doubted. The origin of this doubt was the emotional perturbation consequent on the changes and disappointments around him and, indeed, within him. Not only, then, was his mind disturbed, but his whole being was aware of spiritual disequilibrium. In this mood and with this mind, he took up those tasks which for so long he had set himself—the composition of a great poem and the compilation of a treatise on Christian doctrine. His intellect, now restless in new things, sternly logical and adventurous in logic, but not profoundly philosophical, travelled along many paths of argument and made startling discoveries. Many of these arguments and discoveries lay to hand in contemporary thought. He took them and made them his own.

When the treatise was done—I think some time after the Restoration, but if we date it at the Restoration my argument is unaffected—he thought that he had sifted matter of belief from matter of opinion. He was, perhaps, for a while content with his conclusions. The truth was, however, that his mind had merely visited certain opinions, known them for what they were, recognized their place in the system he was making for himself; but it had not dwelt there. They did not satisfy the needs of his spirit: they seemed only to satisfy his mind. He came to realize that 'it is a humane frailty to err, and no man is infallible here on earth'. (vi. 168.) His greatest audacities, he knew, were not 'necessary to salvation'. His departures from orthodoxy were mere 'neighbouring differences'.

No man's spirit is really nourished on argument, although we can very often detect the needs of that spirit in the things he argues about. We can detect, too, the perturbation of spirit in the very need for argument. So it is with Milton. The discrepancies between the treatise and the poems, the very temper in which *Paradise Regained* and *Samson Agonistes* were written, show that *De Doctrina Christiana* is to some extent—may I use the word?—merely epiphenomenal. Milton's deeper needs and more lasting satisfactions are to be found elsewhere.

The poems report the more integral truth of Milton's spiritual development. They not only tell us what were the achievements of his spiritual inquiry, but they also embody the affections of his heart, his agonies, his inward struggles, during the very process of inquiry. In so far as a system of doctrine gives to them their anatomy, two things must be borne in mind. First, those elements in that system will receive emphasis which answer the deepest needs of the poet's imagination and, hence, of his spirit. Secondly, a man does not write a poem like *Paradise Lost* without experiencing some profound change in his mind and heart. The poem is determined by and itself determines a changing religious outlook. It arises out of Milton's quarrel with himself, but it does not leave that quarrel unaffected. His affection towards God, his assurance of man's free-will were surely transformed in the process of composition. His understanding of Christian experience was re-fashioned. *Paradise Lost* not only reports the change, it is itself a part of the process of change in Milton's religious views.

*De Doctrina Christiana* contains the fruits of Milton's intellectual search for a way of reconciliation between man and God. *Paradise Lost* is the expression of a spirit, disturbed in its relation with God, filling high argument with passionate experience. There is no epilogue to the treatise to gather up the threads and make clear what satisfaction, what integrated form of faith, if any, Milton was able to fashion for himself. All we have is the dry logic and the passages from scripture with which Milton defends the individual points of his unorthodox beliefs. To *Paradise Lost*, there is both a sequel and an epilogue, *Paradise Regained* and *Samson Agonistes*. In these may be read the wisdom, the calm, the submission even which followed the doubts and the spiritual conflict out of which were

born the treatise and the earlier books of the longer
poem.

## II

I first of all present what evidence leads me to
believe that the early books of *Paradise Lost* were
written before Milton framed certain of the arguments in *De Doctrina Christiana*.

The most important question to decide is whether
or not Milton was anti-Trinitarian when he composed *Paradise Lost*. The view I shall put forward is
that Milton was Trinitarian when the early books
were composed, but that his Trinitarianism is
yielding to the pressure of other opinion in the later
books.

To show Milton to be anti-Trinitarian requires
something more than evidence that he implied in
some degree the subordination of the Son to the
Father; for such subordination is recognized in all
scholastic theology. In the *Quicunque Vult*, for
example, occurs the phrase: 'minor Patre secundum
humanitatem'. The specific marks of Milton's later
view, as argued in *De Doctrina Christiana*, are these:
the Son is different from the Father in essence as well
as in substance; the Son was generated in time in
pursuance of God's decree—that is to say, the Son
is a creature.

The references to the Son in *Paradise Lost*
generally agree with statements made by Calvin in
his *Institutes*. Referring to Heb. i. 3 ('Who being
the brightness of his glory, and the express image of
his person') Calvin stated that 'the Father, though
distinguished by his own peculiar properties, has

expressed himself wholly in his Son' and that 'the fair inference from the Apostle's words is that there is a proper subsistence (hypostasis) of the Father which shines refulgent in the Son'.[1] Milton's view of the Son is precisely parallel to this:

> . . . on his right
> The radiant image of his Glory sat. (iii. 62.)

> . . . in him all his Father shon
> *Substantially express'd,* and in his face
> Divine compassion visibly appeerd. (iii. 139.)

> In whose conspicuous count'nance . . .
> . . . th' Almighty Father shines . . .
>    . . . on thee
> Impresst the effulgence of his Glorie abides. (iii. 385.)

There are, moreover, passages in *Paradise Lost* which seem to imply on Milton's part a desire to emphasize the fact that the Son is equal to the Father, and it is hardly possible to reconcile these passages with the arguments in Chapter V, 'De Filio', in the treatise. The Son is spoken of as

> Equal to God, and equally enjoying
> God-like fruition. (iii. 306.)

In Book VII, the Father consults with the Son:

> Let us make now Man in our image, Man
> In our similitude. (vii. 519–20.)

[1] Calvin, *Institutes,* Edinburgh, 1845, i, 147.

In Book VI, the Son addresses the Father in words which seem to imply a certain reciprocity unthinkable in terms of the views set out in the treatise:

> O Father, O Supream of heav'nly Thrones,
> First, Highest, Holiest, Best, thou alwayes seekst
> To glorifie thy Son, I alwayes thee. (vi. 723 ff.)

Even in Book X, the 'radiant Seat' of the Son is described as of 'high collateral glorie'. (x. 86.)

It is possible to quote isolated passages from *De Doctrina Christiana* which seem to parallel these from *Paradise Lost*. It has been suggested, for example, that Milton admits in the treatise that the Son is equal with the Father. Certainly he quotes Phil. ii. 6 : 'being in the form of God, thought it not robbery to be equal with God'. It is quite clear, however, that this passage is inconvenient to Milton's argument. He uses it merely to support his view that the Son is of a different essence from the Father, and he doubts whether the passage really implies their co-equality. In the very next paragraph he begins to show that the Son is inferior to, lesser than, the Father, as God, the Son and the Apostles everywhere declare. Milton's view is stated unequivocally—the Son is in no respect equal to the Father. The very phrase used of the Son in Phil. ii. 6 is taken by Milton to show that the Son is, indeed, inferior to God:

> For " to think " is nothing else than to entertain an opinion, which cannot be properly said of God. (xiv. 343.)

We might allow that this passage from *De Doctrina Christiana* is compatible with the phrase 'equal to God'; but not with its most emphatic sequel, 'equally enjoying God-like fruition'.

It is true, too, that in the treatise Milton quotes and discusses those passages of Scripture in which the Son is said to sit on the right hand of God, to be glorified by him, to be 'the brightness of his glory and the express image of his person'. But, interpreted in terms of the logic of the treatise, there is no parallel to the lines:

> in him all his Father shon
> Substantially express'd.

For according to the logic of the treatise, 'substantially' and 'essentially' mean the same thing. (xiv. 221.) In God, substance and *hypostasis* mean no more than 'perfect essence existing *per se*'. These lines, then, must mean that the essence of the Father shines in the substance of the Son—a view which Milton emphatically repudiates in *De Doctrina Christiana*. I hesitate to push this logic to the point where these lines from the poem would imply that God and the Son are co-essential. All we can say is that it looks very much like it.

It cannot be shown from *Paradise Lost* that Milton had reached the view that the Son is not co-essential with the Father: the evidence, indeed, points the other way. There is, however, one passage which seems to imply that the Son was generated in time according to God's decree. If this passage really shows that Milton had come to that conclusion, any idea that the poem is other than anti-Trinitarian must, I agree, be abandoned. The occasion for Satan's rebellion is God's speech:

> Hear all ye Angels, Progenie of Light,
> Thrones, Dominations, Princedoms, Vertues, Powers,
> Hear my Decree, which unrevok't shall stand.
> This day I have begot whom I declare
> My onely Son, and on this holy Hill
> Him have anointed, whom ye now behold
> At my right hand. (v. 600.)

This seems to be unambiguous, the precise parallel of the view argued in *De Doctrina Christiana*. Certain difficulties, however, present themselves. The passage cannot mean precisely what it says. The begetting was done 'this day'? Surely not, for the hierarchies of the angels, in whose 'glittering tissues' are 'emblazed holy memorials', are assembled to hear the word of God. And these were created by the Son, as we hear towards the close of the same book. How could the Father say, then: '*This day* I have begot,' etc.? There is scriptural parallel for the passage, but not for the view that the Son was created in time in pursuance of a decree. Milton himself points out in *De Doctrina Christiana* that

> throughout the Scriptures the Son is never said to be begotten, except in a metaphorical sense;

and that consequently

> it seems probable that he is called *only begotten* principally because he is the one mediator between God and man. (xiv. 191.)

It is in the metaphorical sense that the Son is begotten 'this day'. In this sense, the Son is said to be 'begotten' when God anointed him as King and Mediator. Milton is, indeed, paraphrasing the second Psalm:

> 6. Yet have I set my king upon my holy hill of Zion.
> 7. I will declare the decree: the Lord hath said unto me, Thou art my Son; this day have I begotten thee.
> 8. Ask of me, and I shall give thee the heathen for thine inheritance, and the uttermost parts of the earth for thy possession.

When, in the treatise, Milton discusses metaphorical generation, he quotes St. Paul's reference to this psalm. So that, on Milton's own showing in *De Doctrina Christiana*, this passage from the poem in no way proves that he believed in the generation of the Son in time. By an effective and dramatic stroke, Milton has enlarged (not improperly) the meaning of 'metaphorical generation'. The Son is 'begotten' and anointed, not only as mediator between God and man, but also as head of all the hierarchies of the angels.

Milton's purpose is dramatic. The exaltation of the Son on 'this day' is an essential element in the fable, for it is of the Son that Satan is filled with envy and the anointing of the Son—thought hitherto to be but an equal—arouses the latent rebellion and pride in Satan's breast. The tale unfolds from this pronouncement:

> So spake th' Omnipotent, and with his words
> All seemd well pleas'd; all seem'd, but were not all.
> (v. 616.)

I know of no other passage in *Paradise Lost* which supports the view so closely argued in *De Doctrina Christiana*: *in tempore genuit Deus Filium.* (xiv. 188.)

The most difficult reference to God in *Paradise Lost* is to be found in Book VIII, lines 399 et seq.:

Whereto th' Almighty answer'd, not displeas'd:

'A nice and suttle happiness I see
Thou to thy self proposest, in the choice
Of thy Associates, *Adam*, and wilt taste
No pleasure, though in pleasure, solitarie.
What thinkst thou then of mee, and this my State,
Seem I to thee sufficiently possest
Of happiness, or not ? who am alone
From all Eternitie, for none I know
Second to me or like, equal much less.
How have I then with whom to hold converse
Save with the Creatures which I made, and those
To me inferiour, infinite descents
Beneath what other Creatures are to thee ?'

It seems difficult to reconcile this passage with others in which Milton speaks of the Son as 'equal to God', sitting in 'high collateral glorie', glorifying and being glorified by the Father, and the like. Milton makes a clear distinction throughout the poem between God the Father and the Son, and here it is the Father who speaks, the 'Almighty'. The Father, then, is alone from all eternity. He can hold no converse except with his creatures. No statement could be more in harmony, so it would seem, with the Arian view, or the view expounded in Milton's *De Doctrina Christiana*.

I cannot believe this interpretation of the passage to be acceptable. When Milton wrote:

How have I then with whom to hold converse
Save with the Creatures which I made, etc.,

he was surely not including the Son with the rest of the creatures. Not even the position taken up in *De Doctrina Christiana* would allow him to do that. If he had had the Son in mind, he would surely have made special mention of him. If the Son was not in his mind, when he spoke of 'creatures', he must be other than a creature; he must be in some way one with the Almighty.

Is it not reasonable to suppose that Milton's views were developing as the poem was being written, that where there seem to be contradictions there are in fact developments? The references to the Father and the Son which tally least with this passage are to be found in the early books of the poem. It is as though here Milton's imagination, not his intellect, revealed to him the drift of his own opinion. He makes a discovery about his own mind which he does not perhaps wholly comprehend. His mind is quickened by the dramatic context into recognizing a new truth about its own operations.

We must ask, therefore, what was the nature of Milton's Trinitarianism in *Paradise Lost* which could allow and determine a passage such as this?

III

The clue to Milton's view of the Trinity, at least in the early books of the poem, seems to lie in a passage which I have already quoted from *The Ready and Easie Way to Establish a Free Commonwealth* (1660):

> which thou suffer not, who didst create man free ! nor thou next, who didst redeem us from being servants of man !

I have said that this passage implies some kind of co-equality between the Father and the Son. At the same time, it suggests a clear difference between the functions of the Father and the Son, a difference, so to speak, in manifestation. When Milton wrote *Paradise Lost*, he seems to have accepted a Trinity of Manifestation.[1] The Father is the Creator; the Son is Mediator, King and Redeemer; the Holy Spirit works in the hearts of men.

The Father is the Creator. Passage after passage in *Paradise Lost* clearly refers to the creative function of the Father. Our first parents are said by Milton

> to fall off
> From thir Creator, and transgress his Will. (i. 30.)

And of the 'powers that earst in Heaven sat on Thrones', Milton says:

> By falsities and lyes the greatest part
> Of Mankind they corrupted to forsake
> God thir Creator. (i. 367.)

[1] This phrase was used in and suggested to me by an article, written by A. S. P. Woodhouse, in the *Toronto Quarterly*, October 1935, p. 138.

Beelzebub proposes that the best means of war may be found in attempting 'another World, the happy seat of some new race, called Man'. Milton declares that this plan was first devised by Satan:

> for whence,
> But from the Author of all ill could Spring
> So deep a malice, to confound the race
> Of mankind in one root, and Earth with Hell
> To mingle and involve, done all to spite
> The great Creatour ? (ii. 380.)

In Book III, when God makes answer to the Son, Milton writes:

> To whom the great Creatour thus reply'd.

The Son is never called 'Creator' in *Paradise Lost*.

The Son's share in the work of Creation is always made subordinate to the decree and the design of the Father. Even where it is of the greatest dramatic importance that the Son should be regarded as Creator, Milton is careful not to exaggerate his work. In Book V, when Abdiel rebukes Satan for supposing himself equal to the Son, he says:

> Thy self though great and glorious dost thou count,
> Or all Angelic Nature joind in one,
> Equal to him begotten Son, by whom
> As by his Word the mighty Father made
> All things, ev'n thee, and all the Spirits of Heav'n
> By him created in thir bright degrees. (v. 833.)

The English word 'by', here as in *De Doctrina Christiana*, is equivalent to the Latin 'per', not 'ab'.

This becomes clear in Book VII. The Almighty speaks:

> and to what he spake
> His Word, the filial Godhead, gave effect. (vii. 174.)

The 'ever-during' gates are opened wide

> to let forth
> The King of Glorie, in his powerful Word
> And Spirit coming to create new Worlds. (vii. 207.)

The King of Glory, as in Ps. xxiv, can only mean God or Jehovah. When the first day's work is done, the angels

> . . . hymning prais'd
> God and his works, Creatour him they sung,
> Both when first Eevning was, and when first Morn.
> (vii. 258.)

When the sixth day calls for the creation of Man, it is the 'omnipotent eternal Father' who takes counsel with the Son:

> Let us make now Man in our image, Man
> In our similitude. (vii. 519.)

The return to 'Heaven's high-seated top', when the evening of the sixth day saw an end of the work of creation, is twofold. The Father, who 'also went invisible, yet stayed', first returned to His high abode and viewed the 'new-created world' to find how it answers his 'great idea'. And that Milton speaks of the Father (ii. 548 ff.) is surely clear, for the 'great idea' of creation is manifestly his (in the poem) and not the Son's. Secondly:

> The Filial Power arriv'd, and sate him down
> With his great Father. (vii. 587.)

It is again of the Father that Milton speaks, when he says:

> Author and end of all things, and from work
> Now resting, bless'd and hallowd the Seav'nth day,
> As resting on that day from all his work. (vii. 591.)

The Father, then, not the Son, is chiefly regarded by Milton as the Creator of Heaven and of Earth.

Everything that pertains to Creation, to the establishment of Heaven and Earth as separate from God and subject to God's decrees, is logically related of the Father. He created men free. He decreed the consequences of the Fall, if Fall there was to be. Though needing no addition, it is he who ordains the making of the world as compensation to himself for the loss of the fallen angels. As Creator, too, when his creatures offend him, it is he who must be appeased—for it must be admitted that in *Paradise Lost*, Milton's view of the atonement is never far from the legalistic. Nor does the interest of the Father in his creation ever cease; for God

> often descends to visit men
> Unseen, and through thir habitations walks
> To mark thir doings. . . . (xii. 48.)

His creative providence continues, so that sometimes he will harden the hearts of the wicked or
deliver them over to earthly jurisdiction:

> Therefore since hee [man] permits
> Within himself unworthie Powers to reign
> Over free Reason, God in Judgement just
> Subjects him from without to violent Lords;
> Who oft as undeservedly enthrall
> His outward freedom. (xii. 90.)

And when the race of men grows vicious, tending
from bad to worse,

> God at last
> Wearied with their iniquities, withdraw[s]
> His presence from among them, and avert[s]
> His holy Eyes. (xii. 106.)

As Creator, the Father inevitably stands superior
in a measure to the Son: not because the Son is a
creature, but because the work of the Son as
Mediator follows as a consequence of the decrees
and designs of the Father. But for those decrees,
there would have been no need for any mediatorial
manifestation of the Godhead. Justice is prior to
mercy, for God's threatened punishment is the very
occasion of Love. In a poem in which the differences
between the divine persons are dramatically stressed,
Milton could not avoid implying the inferiority of
the Son; nor, perhaps, did he wish to do so.

The attribute which chiefly inheres in the Father,
as made manifest, is, then, Justice. This justice
shows itself in two ways: in the inviolability of

7

God's decrees and in the inevitability of that
retribution which follows disobedience of God's
commands. The God known to Satan is an avenging
God, a God who exacts dire penalties from those who
defy him. So is the God known to Adam; but in
Adam's case Justice is satisfied by the ransom paid
for many. Without that ransom, God could not be
true to himself, if he did not exact the 'rigid satisfaction':

> Dye hee or Justice must; unless for him
> Som other able, and as willing, pay
> The rigid satisfaction, death for death. (iii. 210.)

Because it is Justice that must be satisfied and Christ
who submits himself to it, the Son is inevitably
subordinate to the Father.

> Father Eternal, thine is to decree,
> Mine both in Heav'n and Earth to do thy will
> Supream, that thou in mee thy Son belov'd,
> Mayst ever rest well pleas'd. (x. 68.)

In these lines, written in the tenth Book of the poem,
we learn something of the process by which Milton
moved from the idea of the Trinity to the view that
the Son was a creature.

The Son is the Mediator and, as Mediator, he is
Prophet, Priest, and King. While Milton is careful not to over-emphasize the Son's share in creation,
he stresses his intermediary function throughout the
poem. In the opening lines, he speaks of 'one greater
Man', who shall 'restore us' and 'regain the blissful
seat'. Towards the end, he tells of the 'great

deliverance' which shall come by One of 'Woman's seed'.

The sacrifice on Calvary is of central importance in Milton's religious thought, at least as it appears in *Paradise Lost*. In the justification of God's ways with men, the appeasement of the Father by the ransom paid by the Son is not only an essential element in the story of the poem, it is also a crucial element in the thought. There is no need to quote the many passages in which this opinion is amply illustrated.

The Son as Mediator is not only Redeemer or Priest: he is also Prophet and King. As Prophet, he reveals to us the will of God and with God he intercedes for us:

> Unskilful with what words to pray, let mee
> Interpret for him, mee his Advocate
> And propitiation, all his works on mee
> Good or not good ingraft. (xi. 32.)

Everywhere, the Son is spoken of as King:

> Anointed universal King. (iii. 317.)

> The true anointed King *Messiah*. (xii. 359.)

The Son, like the Father, is distinguished by a special attribute. And Milton leaves us in no doubt what this attribute is: it is Love. In what I take to be a significant passage, we are told that the Son is to be worshipped as Love, as the supreme manifestation of Love. For this very reason, his name is to be *coupled with that of the Father*:

> . . . O unexampl'd love,
> Love no where to be found less then Divine!
> Hail Son of God, Saviour of Men, thy Name
> Shall be the copious matter of my Song
> Henceforth, and never shall my Harp thy praise
> Forget, nor from thy Fathers praise disjoine. (iii. 410.)

The Father himself declares that the Son is worthy
to be anointed King,

> because in thee
> Love hath abounded more then Glory abounds.

And Michael tells Adam:

> The Law of God exact he shall fulfill
> Both by obedience and by love, though love
> Alone fulfill the Law. (xii. 402.)

The Son, then, in *Paradise Lost* is chiefly Love
manifest. Not the Father, but the Son, by offering
himself as a sacrifice, could reveal to Man the nature
of Divine Love. Divine Love alone could appease
Divine Justice:

> in him all his Father shon
> Substantially express'd, and in his face
> Divine compassion visibly appeerd,
> Love without end, and without measure Grace.
>
> (iii. 139.)

In *De Doctrina Christiana*, Milton expresses considerable doubt as to whether the Holy Spirit is a
person. His remarks on the Holy Spirit depreciate

his office and his being in a manner which, in Milton's time, might well have been regarded as blasphemous. His last word on the Holy Spirit seems to be contained in an addition to the manuscript of the treatise in Chapter XXVII, 'Of Gospel Liberty'. There Milton has added a paragraph to explain the manner in which the Gospel has been written 'by the Holy Spirit in the hearts of believers':

> By the Holy Spirit: the gift of God, and peculiar to the Gospel. (xvi. 119.)

This addition emphasizes the length to which Milton went in limiting the function of the Holy Spirit and impoverishing his nature. Certainly, in the treatise, Milton expresses the opinion that the Spirit which 'moved upon the face of the waters' may be merely 'the divine breath of the Father' or (more probably) the Son himself.

In *Paradise Lost*, Milton clearly addresses the Holy Spirit as a divine person:

> And chiefly Thou O Spirit, that dost prefer
> Before all Temples th' upright heart and pure,
> Instruct me, for Thou know'st; Thou from the first
> Was present, and with mighty wings outspread
> Dove-like satst brooding on the vast Abyss
> And mad'st it pregnant: What in me is dark
> Illumin, what is low raise and support. (i. 17–23.)

This is a clear invocation, and differs, I think, from the parallel apostrophe in *Paradise Regained*, where there is little at variance (granted the greater freedom of the poet) with the view put forward in *De Doctrina Christiana*:

> Thou Spirit who ledst this glorious Eremite
> Into the Desert, his Victorious Field
> Against the Spiritual Foe, and broughtst him thence
> By proof the undoubted Son of God, inspire,
> As thou art wont, my prompted Song else mute. (i. 8.)

Milton could have written the second but not the first of these passages, holding the views and being aware of the doubts expressed in his treatise:

> He who is sought from the Father, and given by him, not by himself, can neither be God, nor an object of invocation. (xiv. 395.)

The *Paradise Lost* passage seems to me to be an invocation such as is here ruled out; not so the passage from *Paradise Regained*. There is a sentence in *The Reason of Church Government* which is very close to the lines in *Paradise Lost*. Milton declares that his life's works will only be accomplished by

> devout prayer to that eternal Spirit who can enrich with all utterance and knowledge, and sends out his Seraphim with the hallowed fire of his Altar to touch and purify the lips of whom he pleases. (iii. 241.)

In *Paradise Lost*, Book I, then, the Holy Spirit is regarded as a Person, who was present from the first; and, in this respect at least, the view of the Trinity implied in the first book of the poem is different from and prior to the view argued in the treatise.

We are confronted here with what looks very much like a development of view within the poem itself. In Book XII, the Holy Spirit seems no longer to be thought of as a person: he seems, indeed, to be parallel to the Spirit suggested rather than described in *De Doctrina Christiana*. The words of the addition to the manuscript, quoted above, seem to be remembered in the lines:

> The Spirit of God, promisd alike and giv'n
> To all Beleevers. (xii. 519.)

> Hee to his own a Comforter will send,
> The promise of the Father, who shall dwell
> His Spirit within them, and the Law of Faith
> Working through love, upon thir hearts shall write,
> To guide them in all truth. (xii. 486.)

We cannot be sure that this shows a change of view. All we can say is that these lines are at least consistent with the view set out in *De Doctrina Christiana*— that the Holy Spirit is the 'gift of God', 'peculiar to the Gospel', the Spirit of the Father working in the hearts of men.

Like the Father and the Son, the Holy Spirit is clearly distinguished both in function and in attribute. His special office is to guide men to all truth, to assist them in their understanding of the 'law of faith' and the interpretation of Holy Writ. Truth and the Works of Faith are the fruits of the inspiration of the Holy Spirit. And with the inspiration of the Spirit, Milton couples Liberty, that liberty which always 'with right reason dwells'. We see, then, that when Milton thought of the Holy Spirit as a person, he must have thought of him as Spiritual Wisdom—Reason, if you will—made manifest.

These distinctions between the attributes of the Three Persons could not be consistently maintained throughout a poem of the nature of *Paradise Lost.* Even though my account of Milton's general scheme is accurate, the very appearance of the persons as characters in the fable—and this, of course, applies particularly to the Father and the Son—necessarily enriched as well as to some extent confused their beings. We read, as a consequence, that in the face of the Father, Justice and Mercy are at war. The Son not only puts on the mildness of the Father, but also his terror. God demands Justice, but he is anxious to endow with Grace. The Son shares the work of Creation, though only as intermediary. Milton, however, never submits to the needs of the fable without scriptural warrant; and his submissions never obscure the large intention of the poem. The attributes of the Father, the Son, and the Holy Spirit, to which I have called attention, stand clear.

It may be objected that the Father is referred to too often as Supreme God for us to hold him in any way comparable with the other persons of the Trinity in the manner outlined. This objection has weight, but I think it may be answered. There is considerable authority in the Bible and in scholastic theology for an apparent, even a real, superiority of the Father over the Son. Many things are predicated of the Father, which would, perhaps, be properly predicated of *summus Deus*. In *Paradise Lost*, this is altogether unavoidable. Milton has to introduce the Father and the Son as *dramatis personæ*. He could not, even if his view had been entirely orthodox, introduce Supreme God as well. All things, therefore, which are to be attributed to the Supreme God are referred to the Father, in most instances spoken of as God or Almighty. It is possible, indeed, that a certain ambiguity in Book VII—where by some critics God has been taken to refer to the Son—is a result of this difficulty in introducing *summus Deus* into the poem. It may well be that this merely narrative necessity has played some part in the crystallization of that view, whereby Milton came to look upon the Father himself as indeed *summus Deus* alone.

The clarity of these distinctions and their importance in the poem are further disturbed by what I conceive to have been a shift in Milton's opinion while the poem was actually being composed. It would need a subtlety more than the Serpent's to trace in detail every hint, every nuance of expression which illustrates this change. To attempt it would inevitably lead to over-subtlety, special pleading. But the clear impression after a fresh reading of the poem confirms my view that a change did take place; and I hope to show in a later section that in one particular there is clear evidence of this. I suggest, therefore, that Milton's view of the Trinity when he commenced to write the poem was one of three persons, each of whom manifested in their relations with man and with the universe of man something of the nature of Deity—Justice, Love, and Wisdom.

I suggest, too, that the influence of this view persists through the later books of the poem.

## IV

This threefold revelation of God to man has significance in this dimension of time, this cosmos in which we live. God is three persons just because man is created, redeemed, and enlightened. What is Milton's view of God before time was and when Heaven and Earth shall have passed away ?

In Book III, Milton recalls a passage of scripture, 1 Cor. xv. 24–8, which seems to have made a very deep impression on his mind. He quotes it three times in *De Doctrina Christiana* and he paraphrases it twice in *Paradise Lost*. The passage reads, as quoted by Milton in his treatise:

> then cometh the end, when he shall have delivered up the kingdom to God, even the Father, when he shall have put down all rule, and all authority, and power; for he must reign till he hath put all enemies under his feet: the last enemy that shall be destroyed is death; for he hath put all things under his feet: but when he saith, all things are put under him, it is manifest that he is excepted which did put all things under him: and when all things shall be subdued unto him, then shall the Son also himself be subject unto him that put all things under him, that God may be all in all. (xvi. 367.)

In *Paradise Lost*, the references to these passages read:

> Then thou thy regal Scepter shalt lay by,
> For regal Scepter then no more shall need,
> God shall be All in All. (iii. 339.)

> Scepter and Power, thy giving, I assume,
> And gladlier shall resign, when in the end
> Thou shalt be All in All, and I in thee
> For ever, and in mee all whom thou lov'st. (vi. 730.)

There is no need to enlarge on the significance of these passages. Their importance in the development of Milton's anti-Trinitarian view cannot, I think, be doubted. One point must be made in connexion with them. In his comment on the passage from 1 Cor. in *De Doctrina Christiana*, Milton expressly drew attention to the fact that St. Paul said that when nothing remained to prevent the Son 'from resuming his original glory' as begotten Son, he will still be 'subject unto the Father'. (xiv. 353.) Is it not significant that in neither of these passages in *Paradise Lost* is the word 'subject' mentioned? The omission is easier to understand when God speaks in Book III. But would not Milton have allowed the Son to recognize this subjection to the Father in Book VI if that thought had been uppermost in his mind? This is not merely a question of ideas implied: it is a question of the use of words, for words mark the crystallization of ideas.

When time is ended, God shall be all in all. What hint does Milton give of his belief concerning *God before all*? Very little, it must be admitted. In Book V, Raphael tells Adam:

> O *Adam*, one Almightie is, from whom
> All things proceed, and up to him return,
> If not deprav'd from good. (v. 469.)

And in Book VIII, in a passage already discussed, the Almighty himself speaks of being alone from all eternity, except for what converse he may hold with those whom he has created. These passages complete, though darkly, the whole story. God before all: God shall be all in all. Now, in this dispensation, the divine essence is manifest as Father, Son, and Holy Spirit: Justice, Love, and Wisdom. This I believe to have been Milton's view when he wrote the earlier books of *Paradise Lost*. We must understand his anti-Trinitarianism in terms of it as a development of it.

v

Milton's view of God is by no means adequately understood in terms of his attitude to the Trinity. His puzzlement about the Trinity and his final abandonment of the Trinitarian view arose from a deep sense of religious need, a restlessness of mind which could not wholly satisfy itself by a re-formulation of doctrine on the intellectual plane. His spirit in its deepest relation with his God was not profoundly troubled by the 'sophistical notions of tri-unity, tri-personality, and the like'; it was troubled, rather, by its darker intuitions of the nature of God, by its active affections towards God, by its perplexities in what it conceived to be the presence of the mystery of God's purposes. The intellect sought for a way of reconciliation with God, but the spirit of Milton as a whole knew another, a parallel development. *Paradise Lost* is the record of this development.

What is the impression given to us of God in the early books of *Paradise Lost* ?

We learn something of the nature of God from the appearances in the poem of the Father as a person —but we see him reflected, too, in a dark but reliable mirror, in the words and the moods of the fallen angels. We know what Milton's view of God was from our intuitive understanding of the state of mind in which the early books of the poem were written. We can detect, I think, not open but covert rebellion in Milton's heart: Satan's passionate and proud defiance tells the story, proclaims the unrest, of Milton's spirit.

In all Milton's works, two characters stand out with such rich life and real being that they remain unforgettable as dramatic creations. These two are Satan and Samson. And they are alive because they are filled with Milton's own spirit—writing of them, he writes of himself. I go first to Satan, then, to discover something of what Milton really felt rather than thought about God, while he was composing the early books of *Paradise Lost.*

In Satan's mind, notwithstanding momentary concessions, God is arbitrary power and nothing else. God is pure will with absolute and humiliating direction over the lives and wills of his creatures—if he so desire. This direction no self-knowing and self-respecting creature can accept, yet accept it he must. It is true that Satan recognizes his rebellion as unnecessitated, as the free act of his own will. He refuses to repent

> that fixt mind
> And high disdain, from sence of injur'd merit,
> That with the mightiest rais'd me to contend. (i. 97.)

But we have sympathy for him in that 'high disdain' and 'fixt mind', because these are the results of inward rebellion against what we perceive as nothing less—and nothing more—than undifferentiated Omnipotence. Satan chiefly derives his energy from a passionate revolt in Milton's spirit against the conception of God as pure will—in a word, against the Calvinist God.

Two things were necessary for the revolt to be aflame as it is in Satan's rhetoric. First, the Calvinist conception of God must have had a firm grip on Milton's intellect, so that when his deeper being questioned it, he could not easily shake it off. Calvinist logic must have been persuasive to Milton's mind—does he not, in *Of True Religion* (1673), admit that the Calvinists are 'not without plea of scripture' ? Secondly, this conception of God must have been profoundly unsatisfactory to him as the argument of his deepest experience, particularly of his own feeling of responsibility before God. There is a terrible reality-feeling in the Omnipotence against which Satan so passionately protests and conspires. This reality-feeling has its authentic origin in Milton's own reluctant submission to the God reported by his intellect. There is, too, an urgent sincerity in these protests. This sincerity arises from that profound dissatisfaction in Milton which was in the end to prompt his intellect to transform its conception of God. Satan is the battleground in which Milton fights out the 'quarrel with himself'—and the subject of the quarrel is no less a being than God.

This quarrel was surely the consequence of

Milton's many disappointments. The immediate and satisfying consciousness of God, resulting from a confidence in God's special providence for England and for himself, had gone. The experiential proofs of God's favour had been found wanting. Little was left except a deep habit of mind expressing itself in an inadequate logical framework.

This view seems to me to give a deeper significance to the analogy that may be drawn between the fall of the angels and the lapse from grace of those contemporaries in whom Milton had put his trust. It finds a place for God in the elaboration of the analogy; and it works the analogy out in terms of Milton's own dark experience. The angels, like Milton's contemporaries, had been specially favoured of God; but they had fallen away. For them and for Milton, as for the fallen angels, God must grow terrible and absolute, for Milton must think that in falling away they prostitute freedom and enslave themselves.

Satan not only expresses Milton's dissatisfaction with the conception of God as arbitrary power, pure will, but he is also the means by which Milton is able to rid himself of that conception. *Paradise Lost* reports Milton's experience; but it is also itself experience, not the least profound. In Satan, as it were, Milton emancipated himself from the long-established habit of his mind, from the hold exercised over his spirit by the barren but unyielding conclusions of his intellect. In the conflict between spirit and intellect, the intellect is stubborn and not easily moved. To speak out will very often shake it; to write it down and see it for what it is will very often unsettle it. This is what Milton does in the figure and the words of Satan. He finds permission in Satan to speak a hidden part of himself. God could not be the same for him after Satan's defiance has been uttered.

It is noticeable, too, that Satan is not the same after the first three or four books of the poem. The virtue seems to have gone out of him and he has little energy left. After Book IV, he is fallen indeed. He becomes almost a mechanical element in the fable. Milton has work for him to do, but no absorbing interest in making him do it. The reason for this, surely, is that Satan was born with energy and indignation to challenge Omnipotence from the realm of freedom. That done—his reason for being has gone. He has destroyed his own being in fulfilling his function. He has no real place in the scheme of things when Milton's conception of God has, through him, been transformed. It is significant that Milton makes perfunctory reference to him in *De Doctrina Christiana*, and that he is a mean figure in *Paradise Regained*.

In Book III, a certain embarrassment attends the appearance of the Almighty as a person in the poem. God has no divine majesty when he begins to speak: he becomes a rather tiresome theologian. One feels that this is not simply due to the difficulty inherent in making God a person in the story: it is due also to the fact that Milton has little patience with the God he finds himself writing about. His intellect dictates the lines, but his imagination flags. And the intellect is dictating argument which is not thought out afresh, which is not fired by warmth of experience as the lines are being composed. God himself defends himself against the charges of necessitating Adam's fall with a logic which is stale and repetitive. No one is convinced by it—neither God, nor Milton, nor ourselves.

But if Milton, in his deepest experience, cannot believe in the God conceived by his intellect, neither can he, in his intellect, as yet find a convenient reconciliation between God as Power and God as Mercy or even Goodness. In the unsatisfactory context of the early half of Book III, where God is chiefly in Milton's mind as Power and unconditioned Justice, where the intellect has perforce taken over for a while from the imagination, Milton tries to introduce into his conception of God the attributes of mercy, even pity. The effect is as though Milton's heart were making overtures to his mind, which his mind cannot accept. We are not impressed by the Power: we do not believe in the Mercy.

God is impressive in Books I–III only as he is revealed to us at second-hand, and that terribly in the mind of Satan. This is the God which has the deepest hold over Milton's imagination. But the very manner in which this God is reported to us shows with what spiritual dis-ease Milton endured this hold. His spirit yearned to be free from it, and Satan was, in a sense, the great Deliverer. Milton wrote perhaps more significantly than he knew in the closing lines of Book IV:

> The Fiend lookt up and knew
> His mounted scale aloft: nor more; but fled
> Murmuring, and with him fled the shades of night.
>
> (iv. 1013.)

8

The deliverance was not complete. The earlier books of the poem are more moving than the later books, simply because in them Milton's whole being is moving towards a release which his heart demands and to which his mind assents. Intellect and imagination are able to go hand-in-hand. In the later books, the major theme fails to possess Milton's imagination. We do not feel that sustaining energy which gives ever-richer impetus to the rhythms and the imagery in Books I and II. There is only an intermittent lucidity in the emotional intention of the poem after Book V; and now and again inspiration dries up, and we have little more than Christian Doctrine paraphrased in blank verse. There are passages of sublime beauty and force— the account of Creation, the 'mortal change' on earth, Adam's soliloquy in the garden, Adam's vision of the world to be. Each of these passages is, however, something of a *tour de force*. They do not enrich each other as the poem moves from one to the other. The reason for this must be that the mind presiding over the poem is not made up: there is still much for it to discover about itself.

There may be another reason, too. Suppose Milton is following with his mind avenues of thought which do not have the whole authority of his being. Suppose he has been, as it were, diverted by the persuasiveness of his own logic and the superficial attractivenesses of a doctrinal system, newly fashioned for himself, from the full realization of his central problem. Suppose he is renewing the 'quarrel with himself' in another way—by giving rein to the speculations of his mind without governing them according to the full needs of his heart. What would happen ? The needs of his spirit would be richly expressed; and so they are in the story of the Fall. Those parts of his belief which stimulated his imagination would receive rich incidental treatment; such treatment as the story of Creation is accorded. But the *solution*, the 'justification of God's ways with men', would read like the record of things thought, not triumph experienced; and so in the main, Michael's explanations of doctrine to Adam are, if not perfunctory, at least uninspired.

When Milton wishes to speak of Gospel Liberty, of the Covenants of Grace, of Faith, he closely follows the lines of *De Doctrina Christiana*—very often as though he had had the manuscript before him and had paraphrased its definitions. The man who writes a work with the book in front of him writes as though the thought had not passed through his mind, but had remained undigested. Much of the thought in the last book of *Paradise Lost* reads as though it had not passed through Milton's mind. His nerves and his blood have not really known what it all means. Only his mind assents to it. If this is true of *Paradise Lost*, it must also be true of *De Doctrina Christiana*.

Nevertheless, this thought is significant, for it shows at least which way Milton's mind was moving. We can see Milton re-fashioning his conception of God—perhaps not in the form which will finally embody his affection towards God, but at least moving towards that final form. I believe that the development of Milton's view of God, expressed in *Paradise Lost*, can be quite simply stated—God as pure will gives way to God who is both wise and merciful, and at last to God whose nature is Goodness.

VI

Already in Book III, we have seen that Milton, though with some embarrassment, has attempted to reconcile the God who foreknows with the God who can be 'to pity inclined'. Justice and Mercy are at war in his countenance. This reconciliation is never made perfect in the poem. Even in Book X, when Man has fallen and must suffer the threatened punishment, Milton's lines fall into a mechanical march of dull syllables as he makes God comment on the Fall:

> But fall'n he is, and now
> What rests but that the mortal Sentence pass
> On his transgression, Death denounc't that day.
>
> (x. 47.)

And when we see that God can relent, there is an unconvincing note in the verse which recalls the flat passages in Book III:

> Easie it might be seen that I intend
> Mercie collegue with Justice, sending thee
> Mans Friend, his Mediator, his design'd
> Both Ransom and Redeemer voluntarie,
> And destin'd Man himself to judge Man fall'n.
>
> (x. 58.)

God is not to be justified like this. Milton's justification of God had to express itself in terms less legal, less logical than these. We have to find a richer, more positive conception of God before we can understand why Milton is prompted to say (as surely he did) with Adam:

> Him after all Disputes
> Forc't I absolve: all my evasions vain,
> And reasonings, though through Mazes, lead me still
> But to my own conviction: first and last
> On mee, mee onely, as the sourse and spring
> Of all corruption, all the blame lights due. (x. 828.)

In the end, Milton's conception of God will not rest chiefly on argument—but on the sense of his 'own conviction'.

God has mercy and pity on man, even though he exacts justice. But Mercy and Pity, even Love, must be grounded in something deeper in his nature. Milton himself gives us the word for this—his 'goodness'. There are many hints in *Paradise Lost* which indicate that this is the view of God to which Milton came. He uses the word in those moments in the poem when there seems to be least of all the veil of reasoning between idea and expression. When he reports himself most transparently, he speaks of the 'goodness' of God. Adam and Eve · adore their maker and praise his works:

> These are thy glorious works, Parent of good,
> Almightie, thine this universal Frame,
> Thus wondrous fair; thy self how wondrous then!
> Unspeakable, who sitst above these Heavens
> To us invisible or dimly seen
> In these thy lowest works, yet these declare
> Thy goodness beyond thought, and Power Divine.
> (v. 153.)

God's very purpose in creation is to

> diffuse
> His good to Worlds and Ages infinite. (vii. 190.)

Adam himself recognizes this, when he says to Eve:

> Sole partner and sole part of all these joyes,
> Dearer thy self then all; needs must the power
> That made us, and for us this ample World
> Be infinitly good, and of his good
> As liberal and free as infinite. (iv. 411.)

And when Adam has learned of the process and end of all things in Heaven and Earth, he cries out, 'replete with joy and wonder':

> O goodness infinite, goodness immense!
> That all this good of evil shall produce,
> And evil turn to good; more wonderful
> Then that by which creation first brought forth
> Light out of darkness! full of doubt I stand,
> Whether I should repent me now of sin
> By mee done and occasiond, or rejoyce
> Much more, that much more good thereof shall spring,
> To God more glory, more good will to Men
> From God, and over wrauth grace shall abound.
>                                  (xii. 469.)

Milton was beginning to find a true reconciliation between God and man in a conception of God, whose nature is goodness. In these lines, Milton, like Adam, is enjoying a release of the spirit—for a while his mind rests satisfied in the idea that God who is powerful is also God who is good.

That this is truly the position whither Milton's mind was tending may be shown, if we anticipate something that must be said about *Paradise Regained*. In a very important passage, Milton puts into the mouth of the Son the reason why God made the world. Satan had suggested that God made all things for his own glory; but the Son answers him:

> his word all things produc'd,
> Though chiefly not for glory as prime end,
> But to shew forth his goodness, and impart
> His good communicable to every soul
> Freely. (iii. 122.)

Milton came to believe that the very nature of God was goodness.

### VII

There is one respect in which *Paradise Lost* seems to show a clear movement of opinion from the orthodox to the more unorthodox—in what Milton has to say of Christ, the Mediator.

We have already noticed that there is a clear discrepancy between the poem and *De Doctrina Christiana* in the belief concerning the death of Christ. In the treatise, Milton states quite definitely that 'the whole of the lamb was slain'. In *Paradise Lost*, Milton had not reached this conclusion, for the Son says:

> Though now to Death I yield, and am his due
> All that of me can die. (iii. 245.)

This raises the whole problem of the nature of the Mediator.

*Paradise Lost*, Book III, is orthodox in every reference to the mediatorial nature and function. Milton himself quotes the orthodox view in his treatise in a reference to Zanchius:

> He took upon himself not man, properly speaking, but the human nature. (xv. 267.)

In the poem, he exactly parallels this view:

> Thou therefore whom thou only canst redeem,
> Thir Nature also to thy Nature joyn. (iii. 281.)

It was orthodox, too, to suppose that the Son in no way diminished the glory of his godhead when he assumed the nature of man. So Wollebius remarks that Christ assumed human nature 'sine personae divinae mutatione'. And Milton declares the same opinion in the poem:

> Nor shalt thou by descending to assume
> Mans Nature, less'n or degrade thine owne.
>
> (iii. 303.)

Finally, Milton suggests in *Paradise Lost* that Deity suffers death in the flesh, but nowhere in Book III does he imply that Deity suffers death with the flesh. Deity, in so far as it assumed human nature and the form of man, must die as the ransom for many; but the divine nature is not said to die:

So Man, as is most just,
Shall satisfie for Man, be judg'd and die. (iii. 294.)

This, again, was the orthodox view. The description of the Mediator in *De Doctrina Christiana* is far from orthodox. Milton rejects the view that Christ 'assumed not man, but the human nature'.[1] He declares that 'the union of two natures in Christ must be considered as the mutual hypostatic union of two essences' (xv. 269): the Son took upon himself 'the proper and independent subsistence' of a human nature—assumed not only human nature, but also man. As man, he had one form, the form of man. In a word, the divine being 'coalesced in one person with man'. (xv. 273.) The mystery of the incarnation is too deep for us to probe, and Scripture cannot help us decide what effect the assumption of man had on the two natures. But the logic of Milton's view must have been clear to him and is plainly implied in the treatise. If the Son assumed man, humanity was

---

[1] Milton quotes Zanchius, Vol. I, Part II, Book II, chapter vii : ' He took upon him not man, properly speaking, but the human nature. For the Logos being in the womb of the Virgin assumed the human nature by forming a body of the substance of Mary, and creating at the same time a soul to animate it. Moreover, such was his intimate and exclusive assumption of this nature, that it never had any separate subsistence, independent of the Logos ; but did then first subsist, and has ever since subsisted, in the Logos alone'. In his comments on this passage, Milton implies a criticism of the notion expressed in the words : 'it never had any separate subsistence'. He suggests, indeed, that the Son assumed, not merely human nature, not even man, but *a man*. The Incarnation, he says, is a mystery ; but there can be no doubt whither his thoughts were moving.

thereby divinely enriched, and Deity was, so far, humanly impoverished. So Milton leans to the view that, since after the incarnation the Son remained one Christ, he could not retain a 'twofold will and understanding'. He can increase in wisdom. He might know all things, but taught by the Father. He himself said: 'Not as I will, but as thou wilt'—and this, says Milton, cannot imply a twofold will unless he is the same as the Father. (xv. 277.) And when he suffers death, it is not in human nature alone, but in the whole of his person, both human and divine. He is Mediator as God-Man and as God-Man he is sacrificed.

In *Paradise Lost*, Book III, there is no hint of this development in Milton's view. Of the union of the two natures, he says simply: 'Thy nature to their nature join'. By that union, he maintains, the divine nature is neither 'lessened nor degraded'. And Christ is not said to die in both his natures.

In Book XII, however, there seems to be a conscious choice of word and phrase, indicating that Milton is approaching (if he has not already reached) the view of the Mediator argued in *De Doctrina Christiana*. Instead of 'Thy nature to their nature join', we read now 'So God with man unites'. In the mention of the death of Christ, there is no such modification as that implied in the words, 'All that of me can die'. It is (or seems to be) the Son, in whom as a single person manhood is joined to godhead, who suffers death:

> thy punishment
> He shall endure by coming in the Flesh
> To a reproachful life and cursed death. (xii. 404.)

Milton indeed speaks of the death of the Son as
though he did indeed die in the whole of his person:

> so he dies,
> But soon revives, Death over him no power
> Shall long usurp. (xii. 419.)

Notwithstanding the line,

> Thy ransom paid, which Man from death redeems,
> (xii. 424.)

there seems to be a parallel here to the opinion stated
in the treatise—where no parallel is to be found in
the early books of the poem. There is here, then, a
development within the poem itself.

In *De Doctrina Christiana*, Milton sees the relation between his new view of the Mediator and his
anti-Trinitarian position. If, in the Son, divine
nature coalesced with the human, making one
person, Christ God-Man, it is unreasonable to
suppose (he says) that the essence of the Son can be
one with the essence of the Father. For there
would be absurdity in the notion that the essence of
the Son, if one with the essence of the Father, could
be 'hypostatically' united with the essence of man.
The divine nature of the Father must also suffer
death, if the Son and the Father are one. There
could not, therefore, be a mediator if God and his
Son are essentially the same. Considering, then, the
logical relation between Milton's view of Christ and
his arguments concerning the Trinity, the orthodox
nature of his references to Christ in *Paradise Lost*,

Book III, are compatible with my view, that we find there an earlier state of opinion than that argued in the first fourteen chapters of *De Doctrina Christiana*. In brief, the references to the Mediator in the poem encourage me in my hypothesis that the view of the Trinity in the earlier books of *Paradise Lost* is different from that in the treatise.

VIII

Creation appears as the first act by which God shows forth his goodness. Heaven and Earth are the witnesses of 'goodness infinite', 'goodness beyond thought'. What is their nature and how were they created ?

Professor Saurat, in his interpretation of Milton's thought, has taken as the most significant passage in *Paradise Lost*, so far as Creation is concerned, lines 168–73 of Book VII:

> Boundless the Deep, because I am who fill
> Infinitude, nor vacuous the space.
> Though I uncircumscrib'd my self retire,
> And put not forth my goodness, which is free
> To act or not, Necessitie and Chance
> Approach not mee, and what I will is Fate.

Professor Saurat interprets 'put not forth my goodness' and 'my self retire' in terms of the Cabbalistic notion of 'retraction', and he finds a parallel to this passage in the *Zohar*. God, he believes Milton to have meant, withdraws his 'essence' from his 'substance', and the Son, who appears as the Demi-urge, is thus generated. God himself is the Absolute non-manifest, En-Sof of the *Zohar*; and whatever business Deity has with this universe is done by the Son, Creator and Governor. God's only share in the work of creation, according to Professor Saurat, is this act of withdrawal—he withdraws his 'goodness' from a part of himself, perhaps to reveal to himself his own nature, to see what happens.

I agree that this passage is a most important one. I suggest that it requires an interpretation precisely opposite to Professor Saurat's. The phrase

> And put not forth my goodness, which is free
> To act or not,

seems to me to be God's preface to an act, the act of Creation, in which he himself exerts and communicates his goodness, making order out of Chaos.

There are two parts to the argument. First, it must be shown that God, not chiefly the Son, is regarded as Creator in *Paradise Lost*. This has already been done. Second, it must be proved that this passage does not imply an act of withdrawal as the process of creation—but that it is indeed the very exercise of God's goodness which is apparent in all God's works.

When Milton composed the passage, he was occupied with a picture of divided space, the Heaven above and Chaos beneath, reaching down to Hell. This Chaos was the 'Deep', into which God bids his Word and Spirit to 'ride forth', and in which they are to appoint the bounds of Heaven and Earth. In this Chaos, Deity must be present, for God is everywhere.

How should God be present in this rude, unformed mass, where all is confused and hazardous? The idea of 'retraction', the notion that there are parts of the universe where God's power is potential and not actual, where he puts not forth his goodness, is an old one. God is in Chaos potentially, but not actively; and so, as yet, the Deep is undigested and unadorned.

Milton must certainly have recalled that other picture of Chaos in Book II: 'unessential night', where 'utter loss of being' threatens Satan as he makes his fearful way through. Because God's goodness is not exerted there, the Deep is dire negation, darkness, and 'Chance governs all'. But when Nature 'first begins her farthest verge', Chaos must 'retire':

> As from her outmost works a brok'n foe
> With tumult less and with less hostile din. (ii. 1039.)

The present passage is exactly consistent with that description. Necessity and Chance, which have government in Chaos, may not approach the Almighty, for what he wills is Fate. We should suppose, indeed, that Necessity and Chance have place only where God puts not forth his goodness; and this view finds support in Book II, where Milton says:

> this wilde Abyss,
> The Womb of nature and perhaps her Grave,
> Of neither Sea, nor Shore, nor Air, nor Fire,
> But all these in thir pregnant causes mixt

> Confus'dly, and which thus must ever fight,
> Unless th' Almighty Maker them ordain
> His dark materials to create more Worlds. (ii. 910.)

Where God's goodness is exerted, there is the sphere of God's will, there is the order he ordains. In the mind of Milton the thought is clear—when God 'puts not forth his goodness', Necessity and Chance and the dark hostility of the Deep have jurisdiction disorderly and wild. When his goodness is put forth, these must all retire and yield to his beneficence.

What is the Deep ?

If we interpret *Paradise Lost* uncritically in terms of *De Doctrina Christiana*, we must think of the Deep as that substance which comes out of God himself and from which the world was made. There seems, however, to be a clear difference between the account of primitive matter in the treatise and the description of the Deep and of Chaos in the poem. In the treatise, Milton says specifically:

> For the original matter of which we speak, is not to be looked upon as an evil or trivial thing, but as intrinsically good and the chief productive stock of every subsequent good. (xv. 23.)

Earlier, indeed, Milton speaks of the 'material cause' as a 'diversified and substantial virtue', which God later 'diffuses and propagates'. Can this be Chaos ? Can this be the realm over which Chaos holds jurisdiction and of which Chaos says:

> Havoc, and spoil, and ruin, are my gain.

In the treatise, it is an argument of God's supreme power and goodness, that such 'diversified, multiform, and inexhaustible virtue should exist and be *substantially* inherent in God'. (xv. 21.) Milton can never have believed that Darkness and Eldest Night, Rumour, Chance, Confusion, were arguments of God's supreme power and goodness. Allowing everything possible for the richer liberties of poetry, it seems to me incredible that *De Doctrina Christiana* represents in this matter the same state of opinion as *Paradise Lost.* Chaos surely is Evil and hostile to God's goodness.

The picture of Heaven and the Deep in Book II is based on a conception of two opposing principles, ever in unequal strife one with the other: God and Anarchy or Ancient Night. No hint is given in Book II that God inhabits the Deep, though potentially, or that all things are originally 'of God'. There it seems to be written plainly that from eternity God has co-existed with Chaos and for ever threatens increasing dominion over the dread regions of darkness; for ever threatens to adorn with his order eternal anarchy. Milton seems here to accept a materialist view, the view he rejects in *De Doctrina Christiana*—that there are twin rulers of all things, who are ever in opposition to each other; or that matter has from eternity co-existed with God. In this war between God and the 'anarch old', Chaos is for ever on the defensive:

> I upon my Frontieres here
> Keep residence; if all I can will serve,
> That little which is left so to defend

Encroacht on still through our intestine broiles
Weakning the Scepter of old *Night*: first Hell
Your dungeon stretching far and wide beneath;
Now lately Heaven and Earth, another World
Hung ore my Realm, link'd in a golden Chain
To that side Heav'n from whence your Legions fell.

(ii. 998.)

It is clear, I think, that Milton has in mind two principles at war in the universe. This view, as we have seen, he may have developed from the suggestion of materialism in Wollebius's *Compendium*—for there Wollebius declares that the world is made partly out of nothing, partly out of inert matter.

The materialist position does not, however, square with Raphael's statement to Adam:

O *Adam*, one Almightie is, from whom
All things proceed, and up to him return,
If not deprav'd from good, created all
Such to perfection, one first matter all,
Indu'd with various forms, various degrees
Of substance, and in things that live, of life. (v. 469.)

IIere we seem to have the view argued in the treatise: *omnia ex Deo*. The 'one first matter' is said to proceed 'from God'. This, in itself, would not be sufficient to show that Milton believed that all things are of the substance of God, for Ames, who believed that the world was made *ex nihilo*, believed also that 'all created things proceed from God, to whom they return'. But there is a difference between Milton's view and Ames's—Ames believed that the angels came 'from God', created 'immedi-

9

ately perfect', both in form and substance, but man and the world in which he lives were made 'mediately' out of a matter, unformed and undigested, created by God raw and disorderly. Milton says, 'one first matter all', and angels and men are made of one substance, taking the virtue of it in their various degrees.

That *Paradise Lost*, however, is here in agreement with *De Doctrina Christiana* seems to me to be put beyond doubt by a clear parallel between the thought of this passage and a paragraph in the treatise in which Milton argues the possibility of that which is corruptible having proceeded out of God. In Raphael's speech, Milton proclaims a certain homogeneity in all the manifestations of substance; from vegetative, through animal, to intellectual and celestial. So in the treatise, Milton says:

> For spirit being the more excellent substance, virtually and essentially contains within itself the inferior one; as the spiritual and rational faculty contains the corporeal, that is, the sentient and vegetative faculty. (xv. 25.)

In the poem, too, Milton suggests that 'all things' will return to God, '*if not depraved from good*'. So he asks in the treatise:

> Strictly speaking . . . it is neither matter nor form that sins; and yet having proceeded from God, and become in the power of another party, what is there to prevent them, inasmuch as they have now become mutable,

from contracting taint and contamination through the enticements of the devil, or those which originate in man himself ? (xv. 25.)

Without commenting on the further implications of this argument, it is enough for the present to point out that it is close enough to Raphael's speech for us to be fairly certain that when Milton wrote *Paradise Lost*, Book V, he held the opinion: *omnia ex Deo*.

We must now return to the lines quoted earlier in this chapter. This is God's prologue to the work of creation:

> My overshadowing Spirit and might with thee
> I send along, ride forth, and bid the Deep
> Within appointed bounds be Heav'n and Earth,
> Boundless the Deep, because I am who fill
> Infinitude, nor vacuous the space.
> Though I uncircumscrib'd my self retire,
> And put not forth my goodness, which is free
> To act or not, Necessitie and Chance
> Approach not mee, and what I will is Fate. (vii. 165.)

This is, without doubt, the most difficult and most important statement of Milton's speculation in the poem.

'Boundless the Deep': that is, the Deep has no bounds as yet, for no bounds are set to it. It is not yet confined. We are told in Book II that it is

> without bound,
> Without dimension, where length, breadth, & highth,
> And time and place are lost. (ii. 892.)

'Because I am who fill Infinitude': infinitude cannot, therefore, be really parcelled out—as Book II would seem to suggest—between God's dominion and the realm of Chaos; the Deep is within God, or God at least is omnipresent within the Deep. More: as God 'fills infinitude', the Deep has such bounds as God shall choose to decree. God can, as it were, whenever he wills, resume the Deep as part of himself or as part of his dominion.

'Nor vacuous the space': this surely is a specific warning to those who would suppose that the world was made *ex nihilo*.

Then Milton goes on to the fuller explanation. How can the Deep be within God ? How is it, if God 'fills Infinitude', that in the Deep, Chaos and Chance and the wild principles of disordered things have sway ? The answer is that, although God is uncircumscribed, although the rule of Chance and Necessity puts no bounds to his Being or his jurisdiction, he may, if he so chooses, 'retire' himself, withhold the activity of his goodness and leave unblessed and disorderly that part of infinitude (which is not vacuous, for he fills it) which lies outside his self-circumscription.

Thus are revealed two principles within Deity itself, the active and the passive, the ordered and the disorderly. The Absolute is here differentiated. For God to act, as Milton points out in *De Doctrina Christiana*, 'it was necessary that something should have previously existed capable of receiving passively the exertion of the divine efficacy'. (xv. 19.) There are not twin rulers in the universe. There is one Almighty, from whom 'all things proceed', both agent and patient, who fills infinitude, but who may withdraw himself so that action shall have wherewithal to act upon. He may withdraw his goodness —but he may also communicate it, 'proportioned to each kind'. This communication, this diffusion of his good, is the work of creation.

Speculation should become diffident, when it tries to give shape and substance to Milton's thoughts on the deeper mysteries of Creation. But the outlines are written in the poem and we can interpret them. God has differentiated himself. We cannot tell for what purpose: except that we find the hints of it gathered into plain statement—plain but framed for the understanding of limited intellect—in *Paradise Regained*:

> . . . his word all things produc'd,
> Though chiefly not for glory as prime end,
> But to shew forth his goodness, and impart
> His good communicable to every soul
> Freely. (iii. 122.)

This self-differentiation of God results in a scale of being, reaching down from him, through the angels, through man, through animals and plants, through the beneficent order of winds and hills and pleasant waters, through the ordering of the elements, to Chaos itself, where nothing is ordered, nothing as yet adorned. The process in time is one in which all things return to God, if 'not depraved from good'. God, as agent, and with beneficent variety of endowment, progressively subdues Chaos, brings order and peace into confusion—so that, when time is ended,

God shall be all in all. Before Heaven and Earth were made, Urania, 'the meaning not the name', conversed with Eternal Wisdom in the presence of the Almighty. When the end of time has come, shall he not still be pleased with those creatures who have lived as in 'his presence'?

## IX

The creation of Man is the major work of Creation; in him the communication of God's good is chiefly to be seen. Milton bases his view of man, first of all, on Gen. i. 26: 'God said, Let us make man in our image, after our likeness'.

> There wanted yet the Master work, the end
> Of all yet don; a Creature who not prone
> And Brute as other Creatures, but endu'd
> With Sanctitie of Reason, might erect
> His Stature, and upright with Front serene
> Govern the rest, self-knowing, and from thence
> Magnanimous to correspond with Heav'n,
> But grateful to acknowledge whence his good
> Descends. (vii. 505.)

This self-knowing, rational being was created free. He might—had he not yielded to temptation and alienated himself from God—have turned 'all to spirit'; he might have been 'improved by tract of time'. Milton seems, indeed, to have taken the Augustinian view that man was created in a high degree of spiritual grace—and this grace might have been enriched and enhanced until man became like an angel. But he was free to be obedient and free to fall—and he chose to cut himself off from God.

Milton has, first, to solve the problem of Adam's, of man's, free-will. I agree with Mr. E. W. M. Tillyard in his view that the 'whole question [of foreknowledge and free-will] was to Milton not at all academic, but belonged to the very essence of his nature'. Particularly, I think, it deeply concerned him at the time of the composition of *Paradise Lost*. Nevertheless, it is true, as Mr. Tillyard further points out, that there is a plain difference between the treatment of the problem in the poem and that in *De Doctrina Christiana*. The problem belonged to the essence of his nature, and the troubled mind finds unsatisfactory expression, perhaps, in *Paradise Lost*; in the treatise closer argument is found, adequate to reconcile man's freedom with divine prescience.

This difference seems to me to be due to two causes. First, poetry is not hospitable to argument of this kind; it has its own kind of persuasion, and when that is weak and sapless, we are not inclined to be convinced by mere logic. Besides, we do not easily accept mere logic from the lips of a divine person. Secondly, Milton himself is not wholly at ease in the position he adopts. His mind has framed, perhaps, the logic of his position; he may have argued it out already in the treatise. But his whole spirit does not go with it. He is still troubled by the Calvinist conception of God. He could not be free in his solution of the problem of freedom and pre-destination, while he still harboured the remnants of that conception. He still speaks from a divided spirit.

Since, in the earlier books of the poem, the dominant idea of God is one of arbitrary Power, Milton remains unconvincing when the needs of the fable (as well as his own convictions) lead him to speak of man's freedom and responsibility. We are told something of Milton's own mental experience when he describes the occupations of the fallen angels:

> Others apart sat on a Hill retir'd,
> In thoughts more elevate, and reason'd high
> Of Providence, Foreknowledge, Will and Fate,
> Fixt Fate, free will, foreknowledg absolute,
> And found no end, in wandring mazes lost. (ii. 557.)

When God asserts that man is to blame, his assertion consists chiefly of a bare statement of the problem, together with a denial that any dilemma really exists. There is a certain maladroit ingenuity in the words:

> if I foreknew,
> Foreknowledge had no influence on their fault,
> Which had no less prov'd certain unforeknown.
>
> (iii. 117.)

This is special pleading. The phrase—'if I fore-knew'—seems to imply that God, and Milton, are hard put to it to defend their position.

The hollowness of man's freedom is unconsciously indicated by Milton in the form he chose for the narrative. Man has not yet fallen; but God predicts the Fall:

> So will fall,
> Hee and his faithless Progenie. (iii. 95.)

We feel that God, like ourselves, must be sensible of what a poor thing this freedom is, when he must argue concerning it. None has accused him except himself:

> whose fault ?
> Whose but his own ? ingrate, he had of mee
> All he could have. (iii. 96.)

This 'ingrate', pronounced before the event, renders suspect the whole argument. Adam, we must suppose, was luckless and abused.

Although the treatment of this question in *De Doctrina Christiana* is more extensive than that accorded to it in *Paradise Lost* and certainly more adequate, there are correspondences of idea, some clearly stated, others implied in the turn of a phrase, which suggest that most of the argument in the treatise had been framed when Milton composed the parallel passages in the poem. The problem had, I think, been solved, so far as his intellect was concerned. Whether it was ever satisfactorily solved for those parts of his being which lie deeper than the intellect is a more doubtful matter. His concession in *Of True Religion*—that the Calvinists are 'not without plea of scripture'—makes it appear possible that it was not.

In the treatise, Milton declares that 'foreknowledge on the part of God' imposes on man 'no necessity of acting in any definite way'; no more, indeed, than if the future event had been foreseen by any human being. God's foreknowledge, indeed, like the knowledge of man, may come from without (*aliunde*) and the fall of man was 'suggested to God from some extraneous source'. (xiv. 79.) Milton declares, further, that although Elisha foresaw what evil Hazael would bring upon Israel, 'had he never foreknown it, the event would have occurred with equal certainty, through the free will of the agent'. (xiv. 83.) So it is with God's foreknowledge. This argument seems to be involved in these lines from *Paradise Lost*:

> if I foreknew,
> Foreknowledge had no influence on their fault,
> Which had no less prov'd certain unforeknown.

Milton denies, moreover, that God's foreknowledge is in any way conditioned by his decree; rather may it be said that the decree is subsequent to his foreknowledge. In a sense, then, it is not God who decrees man's Fall: man himself decrees it:

> they themselves decreed
> Thir own revolt, not I. (iii. 116.)

God's decree, indeed, left certain things 'to the uncontrolled decision of man'. (xiv. 77.) From all eternity, he has determined to place many things at man's disposal. (xiv. 75.) If he took away their freedom, if he exerted a control which necessitated man's actions, he would be mutable and unlike himself.

> He would indeed be mutable, neither would his counsel stand, if he were to obstruct by another decree that liberty which he had already decreed, or were to darken it with the least shadow of necessity. (xiv. 77.)

So in the poem Milton says that without the 'least impulse or shadow of fate', God

> formd them free, and free they must remain,
> Till they enthrall themselves: I else must change
> Thir nature, and revoke the high Decree
> Unchangeable, Eternal, which ordain'd
> Thir freedom. (iii. 124.)

Finally, Milton argues that if the use of the free-will be not admitted, 'whatever worship or love we render to God is entirely vain and of no value; the acceptableness of duties done under a law of necessity is diminished, or rather is annihilated altogether'. (xiv. 139.) In Book III of the poem, speaking of an obedience necessitated, the Father asks:

> What pleasure I from such obedience paid. (iii. 107.)

And in Book V Raphael tells Adam:

> Our voluntarie service he requires,
> Not our necessitated, such with him
> Findes no acceptance, nor can find. (v. 529.)

It seems likely that Milton knew all the arguments concerning free-will and predestination when he wrote about the problem in *Paradise Lost*. We can only suppose that argument should be much more authoritative when it comes from the lips of the Almighty; and that there is too emphatic a contrast between the God whom Satan defies and the God who declares that his foreknowledge 'had no influence on their fault'.

Nevertheless, troubled though he may have been, the very trouble in Milton's mind arose from his consciousness of man's freedom and man's responsibility. Man had wilfully alienated himself from God. Milton could not escape this conclusion.

x

After Book III, Milton takes for granted the responsibility of man, and becomes increasingly concerned with the blessedness of life at one with God and the desperate condition of those who are cut off from God. This concern goes hand-in-hand with that change in Milton's conception of God which we have already noted. It is significant, I think, that Satan should first discover for us the nature of this change, for he himself is transformed. We see now that his 'Evil, be thou my good' is an empty boast: his 'Better to reign in Hell than serve in Heaven' a desperate cry. Satan lacks the final courage of his defiance, just because in Milton that defiance was but the prelude to a new and deepened understanding. It is in Book IV that Satan loses that vain, proud temper which made him declare:

> What though the field be lost?
> All is not lost; the unconquerable Will,
> And study of revenge, immortal hate,
> And courage never to submit or yield. (i. 105.)

Now he begins to speak of God's goodness, to recognize again the nature of true freedom, to repent that choice which has led him to prefer slavery to God's service:

> Ah wherfore! he deservd no such return
> From me, whom he created what I was
> In that bright eminence, and with his good
> Upbraided none; nor was his service hard.
> What could be less then to afford him praise,
> The easiest recompence, and pay him thanks,
> How due! yet all his good prov'd ill in me,
> And wrought but malice. . . .
> [I] understood not that a grateful mind
> By owing owes not, but still pays, at once
> Indebted and dischargd; what burden then? . . .
> Nay curs'd be thou; since against his thy will
> Chose freely what it now so justly rues.
> Me miserable! which way shall I flie
> Infinite wrauth, and infinite despaire?
> Which way I flie is Hell; my self am Hell;
> And in the lowest deep a lower deep
> Still threatning to devour me opens wide. (iv. 42 ff.)

The nature of this Hell, which is in Satan himself, we now begin to see. The consequence of alienation from God is the surrender of the soul to the mastery of passionate impulse. The eyes, once keen with challenge, are clouded now and the face is furrowed with despair:

> Thus while he spake, each passion dimm'd his face
> Thrice chang'd with pale, ire, envie and despair,
> Which marrd his borrow'd visage, and betraid
> Him counterfet, if any eye beheld.
> For heav'nly mindes from such distempers foule
> Are ever cleer. (iv. 114 ff.)

Throughout the poem, now, Milton makes plain to us that Satan is a slave to passion. Pride caused his fall, and, early in his career of evil, he conceived an incestuous passion for Sin, his daughter, who, fully-armed, sprang from his head. He turns 'for envy', 'with jealous leer malign'. He is 'overcome with rage'. He pours from 'inward grief his bursting passion into plaints'.

Through him—because of what he has not and envies whomsoever has—we see something of the nature of goodness. To see Adam and Eve, 'imparadised in one another's arms', is to him a 'sight hateful, sight tormenting'. And when Zephon speaks to him:

> abasht the Devil stood,
> And felt how awful goodness is, and saw
> Vertue in her shape how lovly, saw, and pin'd
> His loss. (iv. 846.)

Satan's loss is that deprivation of the spirit which results, as Milton points out in *De Doctrina Christiana*, in the 'obscuration (to a great extent) of that right reason which enabled man' (and here Satan) 'to discern the chief good, and in which consisted the life of the understanding'; in that sacrifice of true freedom, that 'death of the will' which shows itself as a 'slavish subjection to sin'; in 'gross and habitual sin' and a surrender to vile 'affections'. This loss is the 'heaviest of all evils'. (xv. 207–9.)

XI

Innocence is radiant in the idyllic picture of life in the Garden before the Fall. It may be difficult to argue the value of the innocence of this life, in view of Milton's many assertions that there is only true merit in virtue that knows also vice and makes a rational choice between good and evil. To be consistent, doubtless, Milton should have regarded with a benevolent contempt the cloistered and protected innocence of Adam and Eve. They had no need to be strenuous in virtue. They were created pure and had no experience of sin or shame. They were like children in goodness—and yet Milton clearly speaks as though their state were high and their spiritual gifts many.

We remember chiefly a certain blamelessness in their love for each other, an absence of concupiscence; for Milton, like St. Augustine, is chiefly concerned with sexual purity. Everything is, of course, delightfully organized in terms of Milton's views on the superiority of man; and to modern prejudice, perhaps, much of it may seem like wish-fulfilment in prim fantasy. Nevertheless, the poetry of it has a beauty which must silence too inquisitive criticism, and there is a moving sincerity even in those passages which provoke a smile. Eve exhibits not only an unself-conscious charm, but also true virtue in her willingness to hear of 'higher things' only from the lips of her husband; in her readiness to attend to household tasks while her master is occupied with his heavenly guest; in her acquiescence in the principle that God is Adam's law and Adam hers. As Milton describes it, this is not merely an old-fashioned propriety in matrimony: it is the very form of what he understands by goodness.

The vision is splendid, but it is inadequate. We cannot believe that Milton admired any virtue that was not strenuous—and this goodness is a little too easy. It is not the virtue in it, then, that really delights him; it is something else. This picture of connubial bliss tells us something about Milton's mind which is of great importance in the understanding of his thought. He is divided. He would like to ground his idea of the good life in Reason and the knowledge of God. But he does not miss the opportunity, perhaps a little wistfully, to indulge himself in a 'good life'—or rather the picture of it—which is grounded in something a little more dependent on his personal experience, a little more related to his own sense of what has been deficient and damaging in his own affairs. Life in Paradise allows physical intercourse wholly without shame and a love that is altogether free from withdrawal or importunity. That God allows and blesses it is well and good; but it is not a knowledge of God that really prompts it. The truth is that if Milton had ever been able to shake off his consciousness of God, he could have belonged to this world; he might even have been of the Devil's party. But he could never shake off God.

Witness how readily he turns to the contrast, which, as in a distorting mirror, makes ugly the beauty of his idea of love. His mention of harlots and the 'bought smile', 'wanton mask', and 'midnight ball' is done with a deliberate (though literary) detail which gives a pitiful energy to the contrast. The opposition, which we noted in *Comus*, has not been resolved. In Milton's description of the good life, as it was lived in Eden before the Fall, we can still discover the divided spirit. If only he could be content with this world!—but he cannot. And so he turned elsewhere to find the nature and the sources of goodness. He turned to God. The fruits of this search—though they never satisfy him —are to be found in *De Doctrina Christiana* and in the later books of *Paradise Lost*.

## XII

There are many difficulties in the story of the Fall of Man, but they do not affect its central significance —that, in yielding to the temptation, Adam disobeyed the express command of the Almighty and thereby cut himself adrift from divine grace and divine favour. Hitherto, he had not known what it was to be other than at one with God. Good was his instinct and neither moral nor physical evil could touch or harm him. Now, through disobedience, he knows something other than God: he knows evil for what it is and good, too, in its difference from evil. He has lost his innocence.

10

The difficulties are many. If Adam was created pure so that evil could not abide in him, how could he be 'fondly overcome by female charm'? Surely no natural weakness in Eve can have made her incline her ear to Satan's subtle persuasions, for natural weakness she has none. The story of the Fall is unsatisfactory simply because Adam's free-will is so empty of moral content. If Liberty is twinned with right Reason and Reason also is choice, Liberty, Reason, and choice must be given something concrete as the sphere of their operations. Adam is asked only to be obedient to one command. He knows no reason and has no grounds, other than arbitrary command, on which to base his choice. He is incapable of moral evil: he can sin only against a positive law. How can he then be free? To be consistent, Milton must have held him to have been morally more of a child than the children of Israel; for the Law which was their schoolmaster was excellent, even if it was servile.

With Adam and Eve, as with Satan, Milton side-tracks the difficulties. The result of alienation from God is the tumult of the passions and the tyranny of the senses. Very well, the cause of the Fall must also be a surrender to sensuality and the tyranny of the passional self. Satan rebels because he is puffed up with pride. Eve fell because she was inquisitive and also, it must be admitted, because she failed in a wifely regard for what her husband had told her. Adam tasted of the forbidden fruit, 'against his better knowledge', yielding to his wife rather than remembering his Maker. So Milton retold the Bible story. Psychologically it is convincing enough, even though philosophically it will not bear close examination. Sensuality is the consequence of the Fall. Logic gave way to the needs of the narrative, and sensuality became the flaw in man which led to his disobedience.

The importance of the Fall lies in its consequences, and it tells us a good deal about the nature of evil, even if it does not satisfy us with its explanation of how evil came into the world.

There is, I think, something more than an analogy between the description of Chaos in Book II—whence God has withdrawn his goodness—and the description of the effects of the Fall in Books IX and X. In Chaos, Anarchy reigns, and the elemental principles of things are all confused. Chance governs all: now Hot, now Cold, now Moist, now Dry, may gain the mastery. In Adam and Eve, passion and appetite grow turbulent and there is Chaos indeed:

> nor onely Teares
> Raind at thir Eyes, but high Winds worse within
> Began to rise, high Passions, Anger, Hate,
> Mistrust, Suspicion, Discord, and shook sore
> Thir inward State of Mind, calm Region once
> And full of Peace, now tost and turbulent:
> For Understanding rul'd not, and the Will
> Heard not her lore, both in subjection now
> To sensual Appetite, who from beneathe
> Usurping over sovran Reason claimd
> Superior sway. (ix. 1121.)

These 'growing miseries' are paralleled without. Discord, found in Chaos with a thousand mouths, known now as the daughter of Sin,

among th' irrational,
Death introduc'd through fierce antipathie:
Beast now with Beast gan war, and Fowle with Fowle,
And Fish with Fish. (x. 708.)

In this parallel between the description of Chaos and the account of the consequences of the Fall, we see something of the larger scheme of the poem; and we apprehend the courage of Milton's vision. First, he sees the Universe and man in grand analogy. The Universe is divided between two principles, though each within God himself—the one active, his essential goodness; the other passive and hostile until ordered by his goodness. Where his goodness is withdrawn, all is confusion and chaos. Where his goodness is exercised, there is splendid discipline and order. In the creation of the terrestrial universe and of man, his goodness extends its dominion and more of the Deep is subdued. Man he makes in his own image; he is endowed with goodness, proportioned to his kind, and freedom to be active in it. But Man, of his own free-will, repudiates that goodness and makes himself strange to it; inevitably, then, he returns to the state of Chaos, from which he was raised, and, should all things take their course, he must be destroyed.

### XIII

How should Man, who has once irrevocably denied God, be reconciled to him in such a way that his faith and his works should once again be acceptable to him ? Milton gives the same answer to this question in *Paradise Lost* and *De Doctrina Christiana*. There are two parts to the answer: God must be propitiated, and man must himself be disciplined until he becomes worthy of freedom. God, through Christ, freely gives of his grace : man must freely accept it.

There can be no doubt at all that Milton never questioned the validity of the sacrifice made on the cross. The idea of ransom runs constantly throughout *Paradise Lost*, and it is certainly one of the most important elements in the scheme of the poem. In *De Doctrina Christiana* we are specifically warned against the Socinian heresy which holds that the life and death of Christ were nothing but examples for mankind. Additions to the manuscript of the treatise show that on this point Milton neither changed his mind nor shifted his emphasis. Why else should Milton, in going over the treatise, insert these passages from Scripture ?

> 1 John iv. 10: " he sent his Son to be the propitiation for our sins."
> Rom. iii. 25: " whom God hath set forth to be a propitiation through faith in his blood, to declare his righteousness." (xv. 293.)

The sacrifice of Christ, then, makes it possible for man—if he is willing—to regain the right reason of which the Fall has deprived him. But he must be willing. As he decreed his own revolt, he must also decree his own salvation. In order that he may do so, God enters into a twofold covenant with him: the covenant of Law and the covenant of Grace. By these man may be redeemed from the spiritual death which is the punishment of sin.

In *De Doctrina Christiana*, Milton established a parallel between the reconciliation of the human race with God and the reconciliation of individual men. The story of the race is the story of the individual written large. The Law is the schoolmaster which shall bring the Jews once again to a knowledge of God, and in the Gentiles there is implanted a law of nature which shall serve the same purpose. In the individual man, this law of nature warns him to resist bad desires, shows him the way towards a knowledge of spiritual good, but never endues his works with spiritual value. The Mosaic Law exercised a compulsion over the Jews, because it was accompanied by a curse and man obeys it through fear. The law of nature is obeyed by man chiefly through 'fear of punishment'. Both serve to bring men to a knowledge of their own depravity so that they may recognize the need they have of the righteousness of Christ. Law is, in both cases, a discipline and a mode of tuition.

This process of reconciliation is clearly told in *Paradise Lost*, both in Adam's own story and in Michael's words to Adam in Book XII.

XIV

The death in life which follows the Fall is both psychological and spiritual. First, Adam is conscious of the disorder in his appetites and Reason loses its dominion over him. Secondly, God pronounces the curse by which Adam is deprived of spiritual favour and must return to the dust from which he sprang. Reconciliation with God, as it is described both in the poem and the treatise, is twofold. Man must first be aware of the need of God and must turn his mind and his heart towards God; next, his whole being must be charged with the wisdom of the Spirit and his inward man be utterly re-created. The indulgence of the appetites will often bring its own remorse and in bitterness of spirit man may turn to God. Out of this misery there will arise a hope that if he abstains from sin he will obtain forgiveness. At last, a new sort of repentance will fill him, a hearty striving after goodness and a detestation of evil; and he will attain a new faith, a full persuasion that eternal life shall be ours on the mere authority of God's promise. (xv. 393.)

In *Paradise Lost*, Adam experiences the beginnings of this process of regeneration, and Michael tells him of its consummation. He first suffers that kind of misery which Milton terms the 'secondary species of repentance'. (xv. 359.) This repentance is prompted partly by the fear of death.

> What better can we do, then to the place
> Repairing where he judg'd us, prostrate fall
> Before him reverent, and there confess
> Humbly our faults, and pardon beg, with tears
> Watering the ground, and with our sighs the Air
> Frequenting, sent from hearts contrite, in sign
> Of sorrow unfeign'd, and humiliation meek. (x. 1086.)

This significant return to the place where God had judged them is the sign of Adam's natural need of

God. He becomes aware of this, partly because it is man's instinct to turn to God for help in his distresses, partly also because he has renewed his 'historical' faith in God by a process of reasoning. This 'historical' faith is described in *De Doctrina Christiana*:

> Historical faith consists in an assent to the truth of the scripture history, and to sound doctrine. (xv. 361.)

This is the faith that works in Adam when he says:

> Him after all Disputes
> Forc't I absolve: all my evasions vain,
> And reasonings, though through Mazes, lead me still
> But to my own conviction: first and last
> On mee, mee onely, as the sourse and spring
> Of all corruption, all the blame lights due. (x. 828.)
>
> Then let us seek
> Some safer resolution, which methinks
> I have in view, calling to minde with heed
> Part of our Sentence, that thy Seed shall bruise
> The Serpents head. (x. 1028.)

It is his wretchedness and his 'historical' faith which lead Adam to the place where God had judged them. And he watered the ground with his tears.

So, in *Paradise Lost*, Milton gives a moving account of the way in which God the Father (as he says in his treatise)

> according to his purpose in Christ, invites fallen man to a knowledge of the way in which he is to be propitiated and worshipped. (xv. 345.)

For a detailed account of the renewing of the will and the relation between faith and works, we have to turn to *De Doctrina Christiana*. In *Paradise Lost*, although Milton uses many of the ideas expounded in chapters xvii–xxvii of the treatise, there seems to be an absence of emphasis on the more original and fruitful ideas contained, especially in some of the additions to the manuscript. There is also, it must be admitted, a certain reticence in the treatment of Gospel Liberty which suggests that Milton was still reporting a view to which his mind subscribed but which had not wholly captured his spirit. We should have expected, for example, that he would have made more of the abrogation of the Mosaic Law—for the treatise makes it clear that this is of central importance to him. It is a little difficult to understand, too, why he does not dwell on the enfranchisement of the will, which, according to the treatise, is the most valuable fruit of regeneration. There is little mention in the poem of that 'knowledge of spiritual things' which brings forth 'good works' spontaneously and freely.

One reason for this I have suggested earlier. There is, perhaps, another. Milton is writing of Paradise lost: the loss of liberty and the obscuration of reason are his true topics. In the twelfth book, Michael shows to Adam a world in which men are governed by upstart passion and in which, even after the coming of Christ, spiritual laws are twisted and perverted by cunning men. Wherever Milton speaks of Liberty, of Reason, even of the Comforter, he seems to mention them only with the sad thought of the way in which man has turned his back on them. For this is the theme of the poem:

> yet know withall,
> Since thy original lapse, true Libertie
> Is lost, which alwayes with right Reason dwells
> Twinn'd, and from her hath no dividual being:
> Reason in man obscur'd and not obeyd,
> Immediately inordinate desires
> And upstart Passions catch the Government
> From Reason, and to servitude reduce
> Man till then free. (xii. 82.)

Milton mentions, indeed, the promise of the Father to send a Comforter to dwell within the hearts of believers and to inform them of the law of truth. But no sooner is the promise mentioned than his thought turns to the 'grievous wolves' who shall twist all the mysteries of Heaven to their own advantage, increasing their lucre, fostering their ambition, and securing their authority by feigning to act through spiritual power:

> to themselves appropriating
> The Spirit of God, promisd alike and giv'n
> To all Beleevers; and from that pretense,
> Spiritual Lawes by carnal power shall force
> On every conscience. (xii. 518.)

Milton is, indeed, pessimistic about the world. Truth will not prevail in the eyes of men, but 'shall retire bestuck with slanderous darts'. The works of faith will only rarely be found. The world will be malignant to the good, benign to the wicked, and will groan under her own weight. So Paradise is lost.

The last book of the poem plainly reports the state of Milton's mind. He sees a world fallen from God; a world in which men choose not to be free and despise the truth. Many parts of the world are unfit and unsafe for Liberty, and the light of Reason only faintly illumines the shadows here and there in solitary places. Power seems to triumph over justice and God's temples have become the resorts of robbers and evil men.

While Milton's mind may have speculated at this time on the supernatural source of Gospel Liberty, while it may have framed for itself a satisfactory description of a freedom which no human assault could impair or destroy, a more simple and practical problem was surely his deeper concern. How shall man live in a world of this kind ? How shall he serve God ? When all the argument was done, when Milton had made clear to himself the enrichment of the will and the knowledge of spiritual things which are the fruits of faith, he was not really any nearer that calm of mind, that settlement of the spirit, which he sought. He had to compose himself for living, not only for thinking. He had to reconcile his affections towards God by feeling differently about him. It is true that the chapters on Gospel Liberty in *De Doctrina Christiana* are symptomatic of his changed affections; but they do not wholly or adequately represent the important elements in that change. The close of the poem more truly represents these.

There is a certain 'calm of mind, all passion spent' in the latter half of Book XII of *Paradise Lost*. The dominant note of Milton's writing is one of humility. God as a person of the poem recedes from the scene; and one feels that this withdrawal is significant of something that is happening in Milton's own mind. God is accepted. He is good—above all things, good. But he is also just and terrible. We are a long way from knowing him—the best we can do is to try to live as in his presence. There is humility in Adam's words:

> Henceforth I learne, that to obey is best,
> And love with fear the onely God, to walk
> As in his presence. (xii. 561.)

When Gabriel sums up for Adam the nature of good conduct, he talks to him as though he were a child in goodness. He does not mention reason or liberty at the very end; the human spirit, perhaps, best attains these through not thinking about them:

> onely add
> Deeds to thy knowledge answerable, add Faith,
> Add vertue, Patience, Temperance, add Love,
> By name to come call'd Charitie, the soul
> Of all the rest. (xii. 581.)

It is as though Milton cares not to ask or even hope for too much. The world has disappointed him and he expects neither virtue nor liberty to abound in it. Liberty and virtue are, indeed, to be looked for in more private spheres; and if here and there is to be found a man, patient, temperate, and charitable, it is a thing to be rejoiced at. The 'worldly-wise' and

'worldly-strong' seem in great things to be triumph-
ant. By 'things deemed weak' will these in the end
be subverted.

Meanwhile, man must 'obey' and live 'as in his
presence'.

XV

*Paradise Lost* is the poem of a man whose mind
is troubled and changing. The momentum of the
earlier books, the varying temper of the later, arise
from a spirit not at rest, but passionately seeking a
reconciliation between God and man. In the first
stages of the composition, Milton's mind is occupied
with a noble struggle to rid itself of that conception
whereby God is regarded as Pure Will, Incomprehensible, Omnipotent. His deepest consciousness,
too, is of the evil in the world, the turbulence and
chaos in men's souls. He cannot hold God responsible for man's depravity; neither can he integrate his
belief in God with his awareness of man's sin and
shame. He sets out to understand God's purpose in
creation and the fulfilment of that purpose amongst
men who wilfully reject it.

The process of understanding involves, first of all,
an increasing recognition of the way in which his
conception of God must be transformed. God is at
first arbitrary Deity conceived and challenged in the
figure of Satan. He becomes more and more—but
never perfectly—a Being whose nature is goodness,
whose delight it is to communicate his good to those
who will receive it. God is not terrible to man, but
good. Man is terrible to himself. Milton sees that

this is how his problem must be solved, and many passages in the poem attest the validity of this thought for the deeper questionings of his nature.

The goodness of God is manifest in his creation. His works glorify him. Everything, indeed, that is evil and dangerous in creation, extremes of heat and cold, the malice of the winds and the elements—all these are evil because man has made them so. Designed by goodness as the beneficent setting for man, lord of creation, they become malevolent and disturbed when man forfeits his sovereignty. Secondly, God's goodness is manifested in those 'spiritual laws' which the Holy Spirit writes upon the hearts of all believers. To be truly free is to exercise that Reason, which is the light of the Holy Spirit, the revelation of God's goodness.

This is the *scheme* of *Paradise Lost*—but I doubt whether this scheme adequately represents the deeper movements of Milton's spirit. It does not sufficiently emphasize the fact that Milton's conception of God, his vision of Christian Liberty, and his ideas of goodness are all, as it were, made known through contraries and differences even more than in their positive natures. Much of the difficulty of the poem comes from a certain ambiguity in Milton's manner of declaring himself. What is the nature of God ? He cannot, we conclude, be merely arbitrary omnipotence, for Milton (like Satan) cannot endure that. What is true Liberty ? It is coupled with right Reason and Reason also is choice. But this does not tell us what Liberty, under God, really is. We learn that from the picture of servitude, given to us in Satan and in Adam after the Fall. What is goodness?

Obedience to God and spiritual law, perhaps; but—much more emphatically—the contrary to all goodness is the cunning and malice of 'grievous wolves', who turn the laws of the spirit to their own advantage. How does goodness shine in Creation ? Milton finds expression for that; but more moving and memorable is his description of that space, not vacuous, from which God's goodness has been withdrawn, his picture of Chaos. Milton's Christian belief, granted the consciousness of God, seems almost to have been framed by a process of antithesis.

In *De Doctrina Christiana*, Milton more fully conceals himself. He keeps his eye steadily on the Bible and his interpretations of it. The treatise could be and was a more rarefied thing than the poem; and in it Milton set down, as objective truth, argument and conclusion abstracted from the deeper workings of his spirit. The impulses of man are various and some of them contrary; only some of them, indeed, are taken up by the mind and incorporated in this system of doctrine. In the treatise, too, the mind makes recommendations to the heart; but the heart was not bound to follow. To understand *De Doctrina Christiana*, then, we must think of Milton's mind prompted by the deeper needs of his spirit, sometimes accepting, sometimes rejecting the import of that prompting. For it must be remembered that the treatise is an intellectual 'system'; and although Milton's mind was logical, it was on the whole unphilosophical.

# 'DE DOCTRINA CHRISTIANA'

*DE DOCTRINA CHRISTIANA* bears evidence of long years of argument and deliberation, much revision and alteration. So far as the manuscript can inform us, we can infer that this process of revision was chiefly concerned with two elements in Christian doctrine—the nature of the Mediator and the nature of Gospel Liberty. If, as I believe, the unorthodox positions taken up in the first fourteen chapters are the fruits of a process of revision, we must interpret them in the light of the drift and change in Milton's mind, already outlined earlier in this study. In other words, we must interpret them as part of that endeavour whereby Milton sought to discover how man might become one with God.

The treatise both elaborates and develops the thought in *Paradise Lost*. When it is in agreement with that thought, it very often makes a more detailed defence of it. When it develops the thought, it pursues implications already to be found in the poem. Its methods and possibilities are, however, very different from those of the poem. The history of its composition, too, gives it a shape which Milton borrowed from other theologians and which restricts to some extent the free exposition of his thought. *De Doctrina Christiana*, unfortunately for us, does not speak for itself on all matters. It was never framed as a continuous prose argument of

Milton's views; rather does it argue and clarify and illustrate certain elements in those views classed under heads borrowed from Ames and Wollebius. What it has to say, it says now with the voice of 1641, now of 1659, now of some later year—it is sometimes impossible for us to say in what year the voice has spoken.

The treatise is, however, an unsatisfactory expression of Milton's views for another reason: the discipline of unimpassioned argument was uncongenial to him. He was a man with a keen sense of duty and he had a great belief in discipline. He could rule his temper and his way of life to some important end. He would deliberately map out a plan of work for himself simply because he believed he ought to do so. *De Doctrina Christiana* was, doubtless, originally such a piece of work. It is not *his* work in the same sense that *Paradise Lost* in its more moving moments is his work. It is a work of obligation; and remains no more than that. The result is that Milton does not reveal himself in the treatise as he reveals himself in the poem. The thought tends to remain outside him, not always digested, not always his own.

We do not know the story of the composition of *De Doctrina Christiana* in any detail, and we are almost wholly without evidence which would help towards fixing a precise date. The evidence in our possession, however, seems to me to suggest that Milton revised a good deal of the treatise after he had written the earlier books of the poem. The impulses, doubts, and aspirations revealed in the poem may well be responsible for prompting much of the new thought in the treatise; and the treatise, like the poem, is part of Milton's attempt to settle the quarrel with himself. It bears evidence of this, indeed, in almost every argument. It is an attempt to do in argument what the poem aimed to do in imagination. Neither is adequate; but they are unsatisfying for different reasons.

## II

How Milton came to be anti-Trinitarian must, I think, always remain a matter of conjecture. We have insufficient evidence to enable us to trace out step by step the difficult processes through which his mind must have passed before he framed those arguments in Chapter V of *De Doctrina Christiana*, 'De Filio', in which he proved to his own satisfaction that the Son was inferior to the Father, different from the Father in essence, and generated in time in pursuance of a decree. The most we can do is to find the relation between Milton's anti-Trinitarianism and what seems to be central in his later thought.

Certainly, his anti-Trinitarianism was made possible by his characteristic way of religious thinking; and we can say something about that. He disliked subtlety and wordy distinctions in the statement of belief. The words 'sophistical' and 'scholastic' are often used by him as terms of abuse. In *Of True Religion*, he specifically complains of the 'scholastic notions', the 'sophistical subtleties' of the terms 'trinity', 'triniunity', 'coessentiality', and the like. This forthrightness in his thought appears constantly in *De Doctrina Christiana*, throughout the argument. He cannot believe that Christ would speak sometimes as God, sometimes as man. (xiv. 223.) He cannot accept what he deems the quibble whereby Christ is said to have assumed human nature, but not man. He cannot attribute to God a twofold will or he is unwilling to attribute to Christ a twofold understanding. (xiv. 71, and xv. 275.) There is, throughout the treatise, a clear endeavour to rid belief of ingenious logic, to simplify it.

Parallel to this insistence on plain thinking, there is also in Milton's mind a kind of holistic tendency— a constant attempt to get rid of dualities and divisions in divine and temporal existences. The soul of man is not distinct from the body, but the soul and the body go to make one nature, one being. Christ is one person, in whom the divine has coalesced with the human. Christ dies in the whole of his nature. Perfect essence is perfect substance, and it is absurd to suppose that perfect essence could be two or three substances. God is One—one in essence and in substance.

This conception of undivided 'wholes', however, is 'holistic' in another sense. Milton sees each 'whole' as a part of a larger whole. He likes to get rid of what may be called 'incidentalism' in his view of the cosmos; he likes to regard it as a continuous process. So in man the soul is not created specially at birth: the soul is contained in the seed. Consequently, there is a spiritual solidarity in the race of men which involves them all in original sin. The vegetative, the animal, the rational are not all distinct and separate: they are manifestations of a scale of being, they are all contained within spirit. Man is not either in a state of grace or out of it: he is called in every moment of his being, and regeneration is a continuous process, a continuous progress. Regenerate men become 'members of Christ', are ingrafted in him, become one with him. In the end, God shall be 'all in all'. Doubtless, too, this way of thought had something to do with Milton's view: *omnia ex Deo*.

The mind that thought in this way, then, was presented with the problem: How is man related to God? How shall he become one with God? In his answer Milton seems to have stressed two things—first, there is one God, from whom all things proceed and up to whom all things return; secondly, the Son is the Mediator, the Head of God's mystical Church, the being of whom men may become 'members'.

Milton's anti-Trinitarianism seems first to have arisen from a consideration of the mediatorial functions of the Son. In *Paradise Lost*, the Son's work in creation is his only in a secondary degree: God is the Creator, but the Son is the intermediary. God expresses himself in time through the Son. The chief merit of the Son, however, is plainly shown in his willingness to offer himself as a ransom for many, and his distinguishing attribute is that in him Love abounds more than glory. The Son is our only way of approach to God: he intercedes for us. In *De Doctrina Christiana* we see, too, that Milton's mind was exercised by the problem of the nature of the Mediator, of God-Man. The discussion of this problem in chapter xiv is the record of much mental labour. How could God become man? In what manner is the divine nature united with the human? What impoverishment did the Son suffer when he took upon himself the nature of man? These questions were not easily answered by Milton.

And as the questions were posed, it was inevitable that another problem should present itself to Milton's mind. What manner of Godhead was the Son? In what relation stood he to the Father that he might be man as well as God?

Milton certainly recognized the relation between his anti-Trinitarianism and his view of Christ, the Mediator. In Chapter XVI, 'Of the Ministry of Redemption', he ended his discussion of Christ's sacrifice with these words:

> At the same time I confess myself unable to perceive how those who consider the Son as of the same essence with the Father, can explain either his incarnation, or his satisfaction. (xv. 319.)

These words were written later than the passage on which they comment, and are an addition to the manuscript in a later hand.

In Chapter XIV, 'Of Man's Restoration', which is wholly copied out in the hand of Daniel Skinner, Milton points out the logical absurdity in supposing that the Son who coalesced as one person with man could also be of the same essence as the Father:

> It may however be observed, that the opinion here given respecting the hypostatic union agrees with what was advanced relative to the Son of God in the fifth

chapter, namely, that his essence is not the same with that of the Father. (xv. 273.)

If it could be shown that this passage, like the one previously quoted, is an additional comment, inserted later into the treatise, we should have some reason to suppose that Milton's changed view of the Mediator came before his anti-Trinitarianism and perhaps helped to determine it. Unfortunately, the physical state of the manuscript makes it impossible to say whether this was an addition or not. The opening words—'Hoc tamen'—used in both the passages seem to suggest that it was perhaps an addition.

This view is supported by the importance Milton attaches in Chapter V, 'Of the Son', to the consideration of Christ the Mediator. He says, for example, that if we are to be reconciled to God through a Mediator, that Mediator cannot be one with God, cannot be the same God to whom we are reconciled. No God could reconcile us to himself by himself. As Mediator, not merely as man, Christ speaks of himself in a way that leaves no doubt of his difference from and inferiority to the Father. When he says: 'O my Father, if it be possible, let this cup pass from me; nevertheless not as I will, but as thou wilt', he speaks in the whole of his nature, showing that his will is other than and subordinate to the will of the Father. (xiv. 229.) Christ, indeed, just because he is Mediator, must be inferior to God—for how should he be sent from God, how should he be obedient to God, if he is co-equal with God? (xiv. 343.) Because the Son could offer himself as

Mediator, he must therefore be inferior to the Father. (xiv. 207.)

What is Milton doing as he develops these arguments ? He is surely arguing the inferiority of the Son to the Father as an extension of the thought—'less than the Father according to his humanity '—as it is stated in the *Quicunque Vult*. He is doing more than this, however: he is basing his anti-Trinitarianism on the very nature of Mediation. And is that not characteristically Milton's line of thought ? If we are to be members of Christ, then Christ cannot be co-eternal and co-essential with the Father—for Christ, and hence the Son, in whom we have mystical communion, must be limited in time even as we are limited, must be apprehensible in time even as we apprehend ourselves. He must, therefore, be generated in time.

Milton's anti-Trinitarianism was approached from another angle. We have seen how both in *Paradise Lost* and *De Doctrina Christiana* he lays particular stress on that passage in 1 Cor. xv. 24–8, which ends with the words: God shall be all in all. On this passage, Milton makes the comment:

> it is expressly declared, that when the Son shall have completed his functions as mediator, and nothing shall remain to prevent him from resuming his original glory as only begotten Son, he shall nevertheless be subject unto the Father. (xiv. 353.)

This is the final argument in the chapter on the Son. I think it was central in Milton's thought.

Milton surely saw the connexion between this

passage and that thought which he seems to have taken over originally from Ames's *Medulla*:

> All created things tend towards God, from whom they proceed,

and which he himself paraphrases in *Paradise Lost*:

> O *Adam*, one Almightie is, from whom
> All things proceed, and up to him return. (v. 469.)

There is no doubt that here we have the very pith of Milton's belief concerning Creation. With logical propriety, then, he could turn from the expectation, God shall be all in all, to the view, God before all.

This view is also given prominence in the treatise in Milton's arguments concerning the inferiority of the Son:

> I would therefore ask my adversaries, whether they hold the Father to be an abstract ens or not ? Question-less they will reply, the primary ens of all. I answer, therefore, that as he has one hypostasis, so he must have one essence proper to himself, incommunicable in the highest degree, and participated by no one, that is, by no person besides, for he cannot have his own proper hypostasis, without having his own proper essence. (xiv. 221.)

If God is the primary ens of all, all else must be derived from him. Since, too, the essence of the Father is infinite, it cannot be communicated to another person; for there could not be two infinite persons. (xiv. 221.) Besides, to generate is to produce something different from the generator (xiv. 311), something that exists independently of the generator; therefore, the Son must be different from the Father and cannot be co-equal with him.

There is a logical consistency in Milton's view which makes it possible to discover some at least of the roots of his anti-Trinitarian position in his whole conception of the purpose of Creation. God's purpose was to communicate his goodness to beings like himself, to make his good communicable to every kind. We find Milton already in *Paradise Lost* limiting the conversation of God with those creatures whom he has made; there can be no doubt that in Milton's mind God made those creatures that he might have conversation with them. It was a simple transition from this thought to hold that 'the first-born of every creature' should be the most perfect created being, that he should be the one most radiantly expressing the divine nature, that as spirit contains body, so he should contain and offer to the Father all those who have faith in the Father through him. In *Paradise Lost*, the Son expresses the Father in his relations with man—the conclusion was for Milton inevitable: the Son was generated in time in pursuance of a decree.

Milton's treatment of the Holy Spirit seems to confirm the view that he approached his anti-Trinitarianism partly from a consideration of the mediatorial functions of the Son. The whole of the chapter on the Holy Spirit is a result of Milton's puzzlement in the face of this question, What function can be assigned to the Holy Spirit that is not more properly attributed to the Son? Milton can in the end find none, except that illumination of the hearts and minds of believers which is peculiar to the gospel. He seems, indeed, to come to the conclusion that the Holy Spirit is not a person, but the 'gift of God'. The Son is the Mediator, and there is room for no other.

When the Holy Spirit is so nearly deprived of his individual Being, it was natural that Milton should revise his view of the various attributes of the Son and the Spirit. In *Paradise Lost*, he had thought of the Son as Love and of the Holy Spirit as Wisdom or Reason. But the whole drift of his thought tended to make Reason the faculty (supernaturally transformed) by which man could become one with God through Christ. In *Paradise Regained*, the Son defeats the Devil, is true to the Father, by exercising that Reason, which is also choice, by opposing Reason which derives from God, and obedience to his will to the more immediate impulses and satisfactions of his earthly self. Man once again becomes the heir to Heaven by Reason—even though he is redeemed by Love. In *De Doctrina Christiana*, to be ingrafted in Christ is to achieve a knowledge of spiritual things, to have the understanding enlightened. Milton seems, indeed, to be at one with Plotinus in supposing that the greatest of all generated beings is the first, which is Intellect or Reason. And Reason beholds Perfect Being as its Father.

III

In *De Doctrina Christiana*, Milton argues that the world and all things were made out of the substance of God. The logic of the view is simple. Not even God could produce something out of nothing. To suggest that he could argues, first, that he is capable of receiving accession, and, since God is infinite, this is impossible; secondly, that the divine efficacy could work without having anything to offer passive reception to its exertions, and that is absurd. God created the world, then, out of previously existing matter. Where did this matter come from ? Either it is co-eternal with God or else it is itself out of God, part of his substance. It is impossible that matter should have existed from all eternity along with God, since it is only a passive principle, 'dependent on the Deity and subservient to him'. All things, therefore, must be of the substance of God: *omnia ex Deo*. God, who is the absolute and sole cause of all things, must also be the material cause.

The place which this view holds in Milton's system is not difficult to understand. He sees creation as a scale of being ascending to God; and that which returns to and becomes part of God must have proceeded out of God—for Milton himself points out that infinite Deity can receive no addition. The view, God before all, implies for Milton the view, all out of God.

I think there were deeper reasons for Milton's adoption of this opinion; and they are twofold. Everything original and bold in *De Doctrina Christiana* is the result of Milton's attempt to bring man into closer and more responsible relation with God. The view that all things are of God throws on man the supreme responsibility for evil. Matter and form are incorruptible—but what is to prevent

them from receiving taint and pollution when they
pass into the power of another party, when they are
contaminated by the sinfulness of man himself?
Man, in his wilfulness, is responsible for corruption
and sin. Matter in itself is good and incorruptible,
for it proceeds out of God. Man cannot blame the
ills to which flesh is heir; he cannot blame the dust
from which he springs. He alone is responsible.

Milton seems deliberately to have emphasized the
excellence of the 'productive stock' from which all
substance springs. In this, there appears to be a
development of thought away from the opinion to
be found in *Paradise Lost*. There it would appear
that God's mere act of withdrawal from a part of his
substance must leave hostility and Chaos and confusion. There it would seem that there are indeed
within God two opposing principles, once he has
differentiated himself in time. Now, however,
Milton's view seems to be that there are only as
many principles as there are wills and understandings. It is these that sin and bring corruption in
their train. To say that all things are of God makes
it possible for man to be at one with God; it also
makes man responsible if he does not become one
with God. He cannot blame any positive spirit of
evil in the world—and it is notable, incidentally,
that Satan plays only a minor part in the speculations
of the treatise. God has given matter to the dominion
of man: it is inherently good, and man has sufficient
virtue from God to make that dominion beneficent.
Evil in man consists of a betrayal of the divine substance by the will into whose free control that
substance has been put.

Milton found that all things were of God, partly, too, because he had a hunger for worth both in conduct and in experience. In *Paradise Lost*, we have seen how he regards the beauties and the bounties of the earth, and of life itself, as manifestations of the goodness of God. Nature itself is intrinsically good, whatever hypocrites austerely say. Only when man has fallen does Nature become ill-tempered and unkind: and the origin of her unkindness is in the wilfulness of man. No better way could be found for the communication of God's goodness than to form of his own substance this world and to put it under the dominion of man. Sin is more than the betrayal of the divine image: it is man's wilful alienation of the divine substance.

IV

Milton's picture of God and creation becomes clearer now. God, while retaining his own essence and imparting it not at all, has by an act of his will differentiated himself in time—so that, first, he remains still infinite, his essence still Absolute, but mysteriously expressed and articulated in his Son, perfect of all created Beings. He is expressed, too, in his creation : he is the underlying condition of whatever perfection works in imperfect things.

But Milton is no pantheist. He says specifically that although Adam receives from God some measure of the divine virtue and influence, he does not participate in the divine nature or essence. Milton's view is, indeed, that in Deity perfect essence and perfect substance are inseparable, and not even the

Son participates in the divine essence, although he was generated out of the divine substance. In the chapter on the Holy Spirit, Milton states his opinion quite briefly:

> That which is of "God" [*ex Deo*], cannot be actually God, who is unity. (xiv. 387.)

God is other than all things in his proper person, although his virtue and something of his goodness have been communicated to all the other beings he has made.

In *De Doctrina Christiana*, as in *Paradise Lost*, there are evidences of two hostile conceptions of God in Milton's mind—the vision of God as Power and awful Omnipotence, as the Incomprehensible and Unapproachable Absolute; and the vision of God as Goodness, whose very nature is revealed in that knowledge of spiritual things, that wise love which are the fruits of faith. In Chapter II, 'Of God', Milton makes a catalogue of the names and attributes of God. God is he who is and shall be, Jehovah and Jah. He is simple essence and simple substance, not compounded. He is immense and infinite, eternal (having neither beginning nor end), immutable, incorruptible, omnipresent, omnipotent, and, above all, he is one. These attributes merely remove from the thought of God those limitations that hedge in all created beings. He is active, however, both in power and excellence, and this activity is shown in his vitality, for he shall live for ever; in his intelligence, for he is omniscient; in his will, for he is infinitely pure and holy, true and faithful, just.

What Milton has written in this chapter on the nature and attributes of God has been largely taken over from the manuals of Wollebius and Ames. There is a clear parallel between Milton's chapter on God, for example, and Wollebius's on the Essence of God. The order of thought and the actual terms used are so similar that there can be no doubt that Milton's owes a good deal to Wollebius's. We have here, then, that 'catalogue of Absolutes' which was all that remained to Milton of his vision of God when his earlier conception had proved vain and disappointing. It would be wrong, however, to take this as his final view. *De Doctrina Christiana* everywhere modifies and rationalizes it, so that it is altogether transformed.

This view of God as Incomprehensible Absolute was in keeping with Milton's earlier Calvinistic belief. Another view sprang from something deeper in his nature. Where the treatise is second-hand and unoriginal, the Calvinist view governs the thought; and God appears as Absolute Will. Where the treatise is alive and adventurous, this other view vitalizes the new outlook; and we are aware of a conviction in Milton's mind that there is a 'spiritual life which is a unified whole at work in the depths of his soul'.[1] Professor Saurat, in his understanding of Milton's thought, has found it proper to emphasize the sterile negativity of Milton's conception of the Absolute.[2] It were better, surely, and more just to lay emphasis on the positive notion of the soul's

[1] Quoted from Eucken by Muirhead : *The Platonic Tradition in Anglo-Saxon Philosophy*, 1931.

[2] D. Saurat : *Milton : Man and Thinker*, 1924, *passim*.

awakening to the working of God's goodness in the human heart.

Milton himself is anxious, in his chapter on God, to deny that God is altogether inconceivable. We can know something about him and what we know is truly known of him.

> In a word, God either is, or is not, such as he represents himself to be. If he be really such, why should we think otherwise of him ? If he be not such, on what authority do we say what God has not said ? (xiv. 37.)

God has indeed 'accommodated his word to' our 'understandings'; but he has clearly shown what he wishes 'our notion of Deity' to be. Nor would he persuade us falsely.

This knowledge of God comes to us from the Scriptures, from the beneficent order of nature, and from the right reason within us. The history of the Jewish race is the witness of God's existence. (xiv. 27–31.) The beauty of nature is the 'evidence of a determinate and beneficial purpose'. The 'distinction between right and wrong' must be based on the nature of God—otherwise the estimate of virtue and vice would depend on the blind opinion of men. These tell us—so far as it is possible for us to know —of God's nature and God's efficient power.

It is difficult to reconcile Milton's clear statements with Professor Saurat's comment:

> Milton means that anyhow we cannot understand God; so we may as well use Bible figures about him; whatever higher efforts we may make we shall understand no better. (p. 122.)

We can understand the nature of God—to some extent: to such an extent, indeed, that Milton could write a considerable book, entitled, *De Cognitione Dei*. God is not 'absolutely unknowable'. 'God is known, so far as he is pleased to make us acquainted with himself'. (xiv. 31.)

God is not absolute, in the sense that he is aloof from his creation. It is true that the Son is intermediary, but Milton continually emphasizes the fact that the Son is only the means; in him is neither the divine purpose nor the divine end. God, not the Son, is Creator in *De Doctrina Christiana*, as well as in *Paradise Lost*. The Son is he, 'by whom all things are made'; but—and the English prepositions fail to make this clear—Creation is 'per eum . . . non ab eo, sed a patre'. (xiv. 323.) The Father is in all things the prior and more important cause. The Son, as intermediary, performs the *express* will (not, as Professor Saurat would suppose, the *latent* will) of the Father. Milton is greatly concerned to point out that the Son is not the prime architect of the universe—he is rather the Demi-urgos, in the true Greek significance of the word, one who works under the express instruction of another. Milton insists that what pleasure and glory there were in creation belonged to the Father. It is God who is said to digest and adorn primitive matter. (xv. 23.) It is God who can produce any effect at all times, whenever he will. (xv. 31.)

When Milton discusses the government of the universe, he is again careful to make clear that the Son's functions are delegated to him from the Father. In his own right and by his own ordinance,

12

the Son performs nothing. There is a reluctance in Milton's admission that the Son as well as the Father may be said—in however limited a sense—to preserve and govern the world. He argues throughout the chapter as though it were the Father alone and expressly who regards and rules all things. The dominating idea of the chapter is that God is actively mindful of the behaviour and destiny of men. The immutable order of things—mutable only at the order and with the interference of the Father—is God's providence, and to God's voice, as to a perpetual command, all things owe obedience.

God is specially interested in the work and processes of creation. He 'giveth the beast his food' and he makes opportunity for pride in the heart of man. He hardens the hearts of the wicked, and he performs miracles so that men may be led to the truth. The same witness of a just and ever-beneficent Deity that Milton found in the order of nature, he finds also in the lion roaring after its prey and in the comfort of matrimony. Milton's statement is unequivocal:

> God the Father regards, preserves, and governs the whole of creation with infinite wisdom and holiness according to the conditions of his decree. (xv. 55.)

Milton's arguments on free-will and faith are incomprehensible except in so far as they illuminate his conception of the nature of God. His justification of the ways of God with men involves this thought: that all things are not absolutely but conditionally decreed by the Father. If God's decrees are

conditional on the conduct of man, they cannot be—
as Calvin supposed them to be—the simple expres-
sions of pure will. Something must be prior to will
in the nature of God, and we must not give to the
will of God any priority over his wisdom and his
foreknowledge. God decrees salvation for those who
live by Faith in him. Faith is at one and the same
time a 'knowledge of God' and the very 'form of
good works'. (xvii. 7.) Without God, there would be
no distinction between good and evil. (xiv. 29.) Is it
not clear that Milton was very close to the view that
the nature of God is goodness ?

Everything Milton has to say about Faith and
Gospel Liberty emphasizes the view that to know
what is good is to know something of the nature of
God. Reason, the illumination of the Holy Spirit,
teaches us a knowledge of 'spiritual things'; so that
we can exercise a truly moral judgement and do what
is pleasing to God. We can judge conduct so that it
shall be held valuable by him. This is our way of
knowing him, for this is the fruit, the activity of
faith, and faith is the 'knowledge of God'.

### v

God is other than all things in his proper person.
He is not yet 'all in all'. What has proceeded out of
God can no longer be God, and even though man
and the world were made of God's substance, that
same substance ceases to be God's, once it has
passed 'into the power of another party', once it is
separate from God. God is not everything, even
though he is everywhere. This must have been

Milton's view, since he so often declares that in God essence and substance are one. Hypostasis, *substantia*, nature, can mean nothing but the perfect essence itself. Substance in God is perfect essence existing *per se*. (xv. 269.) Milton, therefore, believed that generation out of God resulted in the creation of other beings, other substances, other essences.

We tread dangerously when we inquire into Milton's ontological views. It seems to me that all his play with the words 'essence', 'substance', and the rest reveal a mind unresolved on those questions that touch the nature of Being and the Real. The treatise is certainly inadequate in its treatment of these questions: partly owing to its form, partly owing to a lack of clarity in Milton's own views. He was not at all times a coherent philosopher, and it is a mistake to impose a logical system on his thought when in fact there was none complete. There are many difficulties in the view that the substance of God, which is perfect essence existing *per se*, is imparted as the material cause to all created things; for Milton himself assures us that perfect essence and perfect substance are one and indivisible. Milton does not consider these difficulties.

It is clear, however, that Milton thought of God as absolute Reality or Being and of his creatures as having a secondary reality, derived from him. This world, so it seemed to him, was the shadow in time of a Reality which knows not time. Both in *Paradise Lost* and *De Doctrina Christiana*, he suggests that there may be a likeness between the spiritual and corporeal worlds. (xiv. 35 and *P.L.*, v. 571–6.)

There is a sense, too, in which he may be said to have considered body as spirit congealed in time.

The original substance of things proceeded incorruptible from God and has remained incorruptible ever since the Fall. We presume, therefore, that change and decay only affect this substance so far as concerns its *accidents*, that is to say, so far as concerns those forms and matters (i.e. material forms) into which God digested and adorned it. That from which these matters and forms derive their reality knows no change and is subject neither to corruption nor annihilation. This is as much as to say that when God shall be all in all he can resume this incorruptible substance in whatever form he pleases—perhaps in the form of man himself, if man has been made one with him through Christ.

Milton is not a pantheist, because he would never alienate responsibility from man. Man is an individual, rational being—and it is in his power to do the will of God and become one with God. Man is real because he is made in the image of God. He is a living soul. Milton answers the question, What is Man? by means of a grand analogy. In *De Doctrina Christiana*, he insists that we are to believe that we regard God as having said truly that man is created in his image. In *Paradise Lost*, man is said to 'correspond' with God. Just as God, the supreme spiritual being, contains within himself all possibilities of things, both spiritual and material, so that all being descends from him; so man, the image of Godhead, has within his jurisdiction a descending scale of faculties, the spiritual, the rational, the sentient, and the vegetative. (xv. 41.) In man, as in

God, matter up to spirit works, if he so chooses. He is a living soul, just because he is a substance, 'animated, sensitive, and rational'. (xv. 41.) He is made of the substance of God, now his substance; and how this substance expresses itself in time is his responsibility, his concern.

## VI

We must now consider Milton's mortalism and its importance in his Christian doctrine. How did Milton come to accept the 'mortalist view' (expounded in the pamphlet, *Man's Mortallitie*, by R. O., published 1643)—that man's soul dies with his body; that the body and the soul are not two, but one and indivisible ?

The 'mortalist' view is a corollary of the psychology outlined in *Paradise Lost*, both in Adam's speech to Eve (v. 100 ff.) and in Raphael's speech to Adam (v. 404 ff.). Milton thinks of man as an integral whole. The process of feeding, for example, he understands as a transformation of the corporeal to the incorporeal, so that angels may eat of mortal food. All things are sustained by substances inferior and less refined than themselves—and the reason for this is that 'body up to spirit works', and in created things, without body, spirit is nothing. In the same way, Reason, highest of all those faculties which give men knowledge of the world they live in, is wholly dependent for its information on the lower faculties. Without them Reason is vain; without Reason they are blind. Milton's psychology would allow no division betweer the 'soul' and the body—

substance in man is individual, animated, sensitive, and rational, and man, the whole man, is a living soul. From this the 'mortalist' view inevitably follows.

Milton's view of man in relation to God, moreover, compelled him to accept the 'mortalist' doctrine. Had Adam not sinned, he might so have perfected himself that his body should turn 'all to spirit'. The kind of death, which is the consequence of sin, must be the very antithesis of this process of increasing perfection, and what in Adam is spiritual, 'depraved from good', loses its virtue and influence. The soul, which sins, must surely pay the penalty of sin. (xv. 219.) Adam had dominion both over himself and over the world in which he lived, because of the Reason with which God had endowed him. This Reason was the godlike part of him. With the Fall, true Reason is obscured; Chaos ensues, the disorder of the passions and the natural elements; there follows relapse and disintegration and death. Man's title to individual being is the Reason which made him god-like. That title forfeited, by a natural decay he dies. Milton quotes Euripides:

> Each various part
> That constitutes the frame of man, returns
> Whence it was taken; to th' ethereal sky
> The soul, the body to its earth.

'Every constituent part returns at dissolution to its elementary principle'. (xv. 239.)

There is one other reason why Milton accepted the view that the whole of man is mortal—it is a reason mentioned, too, in the pamphlet, *Man's*

*Mortallitie.* There it is pointed out that if the soul is separate from the body, if it is not imparted with the seed, it must be specially created with every birth. This is to impose on God a tedious task, not even, as Milton indicates, giving him due rest on the Sabbath. More; it is to charge God with infusing in us a soul which is 'the author of all sinne'. Milton makes the same point, when he says:

> to create souls thus circumstanced, would have argued as much injustice, as to have created the first man Adam himself impaired in his nature, and destitute of original righteousness. (xv. 47.)

Milton's view of the Fall and of original sin made him conceive of the race as having a certain spiritual solidarity. For Adam's fall, he himself was in part responsible, for he shares Adam's manhood and he is of Adam's seed. He had to believe, therefore, that the soul is communicated with the seed, inseparable from the body both at birth and death.

Milton may have been puzzled to reconcile this view with the immortality of man's individual being, but he certainly believed in immortality. He affirms this belief, and there is no reason why we should not accept his plain statement. In one respect, there is no difficulty. If man is real and god-like, so long as Reason governs his conduct, so long as he is made one with God through Christ, he will preserve his individual being, or rather his title to it—and Milton clearly believes that the faithful are members of Christ when Christ is one with God. But how shall the wicked endure, when the last judgement has been pronounced ? Milton does not solve this problem. We must be content to repeat his own words—that Death is a sleep until the second coming of Christ; that after the day of judgement, the good shall be one with Christ; that if it were not so, 'the righteous would be of all men the most miserable' and the wicked, who have the better time in this life, the most happy; that the wicked are consigned to punishment according to their guilt, and that they are not utterly destroyed—for 'that would be a consummation more to be desired than expected by souls in perdition'. Men are known by God, either as good or evil, persevering or backsliding. I think that Milton must have held that to be their immortality.

## VII

The arguments by which Milton shows that God's predestinatory decrees are conditional on man's use or abuse of his free-will are most of them already implied in *Paradise Lost*. The story of man's reconciliation with God is told there, too, in much the same detail as it is expounded in *De Doctrina Christiana*. The poem is not, however, adequate in its treatment of the relation between faith and works, and the treatise gives us a fuller understanding of Milton's thought on this all-important question.

We have seen that in all probability Milton was for long content to take for granted the nature of Gospel Liberty and that, where he elaborated his ideas on freedom at all, he did so on a psychological plane, and thought of freedom as the control that Reason may exercise over the passions. He had an empirical understanding of the free man, based on his own not altogether fortunate experience. Prompted to find the sanctions for and the nature of freedom elsewhere, he made in *De Doctrina Christiana* a closer examination of the bases of Christian conduct—he looked, indeed, to God for the sanction that he could not find in contemporary society.

The excellence of faith is that it 'gives to God the highest glory of righteousness and truth'. (xv. 401.) This is of central importance in Milton's discussion of faith; God is the source of goodness and truth. Only in so far as we know God, and recognize his nature, are we capable of good works. We live in faith, when we freely choose a sanction for conduct, grounded in our understanding of 'spiritual things'. No servile obedience to an external law, no mere acceptance of the promise of eternal life is sufficient to make our conduct valuable. We ourselves must judge it good, persuaded by our knowledge of God.

All men, whether regenerate or unregenerate, have a certain 'gift of reason' implanted in them, for the remnants of the divine image remain with all:

> the gift of reason has been implanted in all, by which they may of themselves resist bad desires, so that no one can complain of, or allege in excuse, the depravity of his own nature compared with that of others. (xiv. 131.)

This gift of reason is accompanied by some measure of freedom, even in the unregenerate:

> he works in us the power of acting freely, of which, since our fall, we were incapable, except by means of a calling and renewal. (xv. 357.)

All are called, 'in various ways, but all of them sufficient for the purpose, to the knowledge of the true Deity'. (xv. 349.) All, therefore, have some measure of freedom.

This 'gift of reason', however, does not enable us to perform good works, does not really make us free. We resist bad desires because we know them to be irrational, stupid, dangerous, perhaps punishable. But this reason cannot prompt us to do good works because it shows them to be good. Reason in the unregenerate is merely utilitarian where it is not merely negative. It is reason on the psychological, the natural plane, and very different from that supernatural Reason which is 'twinned' with true Liberty. It is, indeed, a reason which enables us to recognize the law of nature. In this respect, its workings are parallel to that fear of the curse which made the Israelites obey the Mosaic Law. It has nothing to do with 'right reason' or 'conscience', the effect of faith. Milton strongly argues the efficacy of this reason; but it is only valid *so far*. Had he abandoned it, it is difficult to see where he could have found any hope for man at all; there must be in man some faculty which makes him ready and willing to turn to God, which prevents him from becoming wholly depraved. But experience has taught him that this faculty is weak and wavering, and that men easily neglect it.

True Liberty, true value in conduct can only be grounded in a knowledge of spiritual things, in faith in God. This knowledge is not given to man by the natural reason: no amount of argument will discover it for him. The true illumination of the mind comes from those supernatural faculties which are infused into the regenerate from above. The passage in which Milton declares this view is an addition to the manuscript of the treatise in a later hand—and we may be sure that it was for him an enrichment of the earlier thought. The effect of regeneration is an utterly new state of mind in which man is able to make his own judgement of what is the will of God, simply because through faith he knows something of the nature of God. Goodness is now chosen by his understanding and implicit in his will: it cannot help but manifest itself in good works.

The difference between the unregenerate and the regenerate states, then, is a difference between life lived on the natural plane and life lived on the supernatural. Milton makes admissions which seem at first to obscure the distinction between the two states. He asserts, for example, that the life of the regenerate man is still a struggle between the spirit and the flesh:

> That a real believer, however, may fall irrecoverably, the same apostle shows (2 Pet. ii. 18: 'they allure through the lusts of the flesh, through much wantonness, those that were clean escaped from them who live in error'). (xvi. 83.)

Regeneration is possible to those who know nothing of Christ, whether they be Jews or Gentiles. (xv. 349.) God calls us, regenerate and unregenerate, in every moment of our living. (Book I, chap. xvii, *passim*.)

These admissions seem only to obscure the distinction: for Milton it was plain. The unregenerate man may resist evil passions and the impulses of the flesh, he may obey all the commandments, he may even love his neighbour as himself; but if he does these things without an understanding of their spiritual worth, they are done in vain. It is true that the divine image is never wholly extinguished in us, and there is, consequently, a spiritual element in all our works: no man is wholly unregenerate, just as no man is irrecoverably regenerate. But the distinction between the unregenerate and the regenerate states is one discovered in the quality of action. It is an activity of the regenerated faculties in man, when something is done with a 'comprehension of spiritual things', when a 'sense of divine love' brings forth 'good works spontaneously and freely'. (xvi. 9.) The act of an unregenerate man —or of faculties not supernaturally awakened—has no such comprehension, no sense of divine love; and hence no such freedom.

In Milton's view, there seem to be two aspects of works—the natural and the supernatural, the utilitarian and the spiritual. We may take a course of action because it pays to do so—to escape punishment, perhaps, or to avoid chaos of mind and heart. We may act as we believe God would have us act, because of the promise of eternal life, and we may congratulate ourselves on the reward offered for good works. Such conduct is merely utilitarian and has no spiritual worth. Conduct that is truly valuable must be judged to be so without reference to reward or punishment. The promise does not determine faith: we must believe on the authority of the promise alone.

Milton's insistence on the abrogation of the whole Mosaic Law is seen in a clearer light when we view it in relation to his conception of Christian Liberty and spiritual value. The works of the Law are not the fruits of a mind and heart habitually and freely aware of spiritual things: they are the fruits of a servile obedience and a fear of the curse. The authority of the Law is external; and our observance of it is utilitarian. The essential ingredient of faith is lacking in the works of the Law, and we do not recognize those works as pleasing to God, because we ourselves have found them good. We are commanded to do them, and we act merely on the authority of a command. The items of the Law are the terms of our bondage.

Similarly, the law of nature belongs to the utilitarian plane until it is renewed and transformed by the working of the Holy Spirit in our minds. It is certainly useful to control our passions and to organize our appetites; and to do so is a necessary prerequisite for the beginnings of faith. To this end the gift of natural reason has been implanted in all of us. Resistance to bad desires may be a kind of morality—but morality without God is vain. In *De Doctrina Christiana*, Milton is careful to distinguish between a truly 'regenerate and Christian purity' of life and a 'mere outward and philosophical morality'. So also in *Paradise Lost*, he denies both to Law and morality the power of justifying man towards God:

> which the Law by Ceremonies
> Cannot appease, nor Man the moral part
> Perform, and not performing cannot live. (xii. 298.)

On man's part, there is only one mode of justification: 'to walk as ever in his presence'.

It was, perhaps, inevitable that the man who had once been busy in public affairs and eager to give service to his country should turn away from natural utilities, from merely human conceptions of worth, when the civil state to which he had ever looked forward was utterly frustrated and the temper of men from whom he expected much proved slavish and pliable. Milton had suffered. He sought consolation—who shall doubt it ?—in the darkness of those years from the 'knowledge of spiritual things'. The chapters on Faith in *De Doctrina Christiana*—and especially the additions to the manuscript—are the records of what consolation he found. *Paradise Regained* and *Samson Agonistes* seem to show that he did not find final comfort in argument of this kind.

VIII

In Thomas Edwards's *Gangræna*, most of Milton's heresies are named. Whatever may have been Milton's deepest reasons for subscribing to them, it is certain that he found each of them formulated and defended elsewhere. Milton's problems were rooted in his psychological history; but they were not peculiar to himself. They were such as men of his own age might help him to answer; and *De Doctrina Christiana* must take its place in the development of seventeenth-century English thought. It seems to me that, although there was much in his temper foreign to the Cambridge

Platonists, he is indebted to some of them for the formulation of certain of his beliefs.

Milton, I believe, came very close to that view of God which holds his nature to be goodness, which cannot accept the Calvinist conception of God as pure will, and which believes that something, righteousness, wisdom, or goodness, is prior to will in God. Cudworth, perhaps the greatest of the Cambridge Platonists, in a sermon preached before the House of Commons in 1647, described his conception of Deity in these words:

> Now, I say, the very proper Character, and Essentiall Tincture of God himself, is nothing else but *Goodnesse*.
> And it is another mistake which sometimes we have of God, by shaping him out according to the Model of our selves, when we make him nothing but a *blind, dark, impetuous Self will*, running through the world; such as we our selves are . . .that have not the Ballast of *absolute goodnesse* to poize and settle us.

For Cudworth, the will of God is always free, 'tho' not always indifferent',

> since it is its greatest perfection to be determined by infinite wisdom and infinite goodness.[1]

This same argument lies behind Milton's consideration of Predestination and the divine decrees. God's will is not prior to his wisdom and his foreknowledge. If, indeed, we are to apply to God our own mode of understanding him, we must believe that he

---

[1] Quoted by Muirhead : op. cit., p. 50.

'decreed everything according to his infinite wisdom by virtue of his foreknowledge'. (xiv. 81.) So soon as Milton abandoned the Calvinist notion of God's 'pure will' and denied that God's decrees were absolute, he approached very nearly to agreement with Cudworth's view. God's will, though free, is not indifferent: it is determined by his wisdom and his goodness.

Milton's anti-Trinitarian view is strikingly parallel to Cudworth's remarks on the Platonic Trinity. Like Milton, Cudworth was deeply impressed by the passage in 1 Cor. xv. in which it is said that 'God shall be all in all'. In a sermon preached in Lincoln's Inn, 1664, Cudworth laid special emphasis on this passage, and gave it a central place in the thought of the whole sermon. This emphasis seems to imply exactly that inferiority of the Son to the Father which is first suggested in *Paradise Lost* and elaborately argued in *De Doctrina Christiana*.

It is true that Cudworth does not openly confess the 'Christian Platonist's' view of the Trinity as his own; but there is little doubt that his 'Christian Platonist' who defends an unorthodox position is Cudworth himself. Like Milton, he follows the Plotinian view in supposing that beings are generated from the One who is God in a descending progression, and that these return towards God, their origin, in an ascending progression. Cudworth quotes Plotinus as saying:

That which is generated or emaneth immediately from the first and highest Being, is not the very same thing

13

with it, as if it were nothing but that repeated again and ingeminated; and as it is not the same, so neither can it be better than it.[1]

In a reference to Plotinus, too, Cudworth refers to the Son [2] as Intellect, which 'beholds Being as its Father'. So Milton declares that the generator must produce something different from himself, not equal with himself. So, too, as I believe, Milton thought of the Son as Reason, the manifestation in time of the nature of the Father.

There is a clear correspondence between the view of Cudworth and the implication of Milton's remarks on the origin and nature of created things. Cudworth believed that the world was not created *ex nihilo*. He is in agreement with Milton when he says that since 'no effect can possibly transcend its cause', the very possibility of an ascent to God, of becoming one with God, involves also the 'emergence' of things, not only from but also 'out of' God. Like Milton, he argues that since God is infinite, he cannot 'receive any accession whatever.' (xv. 27.) Cudworth says that the material cause was therefore either God or nothing: nothing can be the cause of nothing. Nothing can give what it hath not. (op. cit., iii. 80–1.)

So Milton:

Therefore the material cause must be either God or nothing: Now nothing is no cause at all. (xv. 21.)

[1] Cudworth: *True Intellectual System*, tr. Harrison, 1845, ii. 391.
[2] *Ibid.* ii. 390.

Both Cudworth and Milton consider the case for Cartesian dualism—and both reject it. Matter for both of them is *ex Deo*.

Milton agrees with Whichcote and Cudworth on the reason for the creation of the world. He states his view quite unambiguously:

> since his word all things produc'd,
> Though chiefly not for glory as prime end,
> But to shew forth his goodness, and impart
> His good communicable to every soul
> Freely; of whom what could he less expect
> Then glory and benediction, that is thanks. (iii. 122.)

Whichcote's and Cudworth's views are identical with this—and we should note that the Son, in *Paradise Regained*, is answering Satan's statement of the more orthodox thought. Milton gives special emphasis to a view which he knows to be other than the one commonly accepted.

Where Milton describes the way in which man may give glory to God,

> glory and benediction, that is thanks,

Whichcote says,

> To be thankful, and to be sensible that we are beholden, and that we receive from God; this is to give glory to God.[1]

Milton's answer to the question—Why did God

---

[1] *Collected Works* ,Aberdeen, 1751, ii. 90.

create the world ?—is exactly paralleled by Cudworth, who says:

> That the reason why God made the world, was from his
> overflowing and communicative goodness, that there
> might be other beings also happy besides him, and enjoy
> themselves. (op. cit., iii. 486–7.)

And Cudworth is aware, like Milton, that in giving
this reason, he must say nothing to lessen the glory
of God:

> Nor does this at all clash with God's making of the
> world for his own glory and honour . . . God did
> not make the world merely to ostentate his skill and
> power, but to communicate his goodness, which is
> chiefly and properly his glory. (loc. cit.)

So Cudworth, like Milton, believed that the method
of creation was a putting-forth of God's goodness,
proportionate to each kind of creature:

> Gods *Power* displaied in the World, is nothing but his
> Goodnesse strongly reaching all things, from heighth
> to depth . . . and irresistibly imparting it self to
> every thing according to those severall degrees in which
> it is capable of it. (Sermon, preached before the House
> of Commons, 1647.)

So Milton believed that God imparted to his
creatures not part of his essence, indeed, but 'that
measure of the divine virtue or influence, which
was commensurate to the capabilities of the
recipient'. (xv. 39.)

We have seen that Milton held that there is a

scale of being, leading up to God, who contains within himself all possibilities of things. Does not Cudworth express Milton's own thought, when he speaks of a 'climbing stairs of entity and perfection', leading from matter to the subtlest forms of spiritual life, up to God ?:

> There is unquestionably [says Cudworth] a scale or ladder of nature, and degrees of perfection and entity one above another, as of life, sense, and cogitation, above dead, senseless, and unthinking matter. . . . Wherefore there being plainly a scale or ladder of entity, the order of things was unquestionably, in way of descent, from higher perfection downward to lower . . . but as the foot, bottom, or lowest round thereof is stupid and senseless matter, devoid of all life and understanding, so is the head, top, and summity of it a perfect omnipotent Being, comprehending itself, and all possibilities of things. (op. cit., iii. 434.)

This seems to me to be the view towards which Milton's mind, both in *Paradise Lost* and *De Doctrina Christiana*, everywhere tends.

Finally, in his discussion of Faith and Works, in his emphasis on Reason and Liberty, Milton approaches very closely to this movement of thought in his own time. One of the most important aspects of Cambridge Platonism is its identification of right reason with the voice of the Lord. In one of his aphorisms, Whichcote defines his position in these words:

> To go against *Reason*, is to go against *God*: it is the self same thing, to do that which the Reason of the Case doth require ; and that which God Himself doth

appoint: Reason is the *Divine* Governor of Man's Life; it is the very Voice of God.[1]

Whichcote shows, too, Milton's understanding of that Chaos which ensues when Reason is obscured:

> . . . it is the weakness and folly of degenerate, impotent and apostate creatures, *to do what is next*: and they are fools and madmen that do only what is next hand; that do not design, do not foresee, have not first a prospect of the reason of things.[2]

And Whichcote's description of true faith is closely parallel to Milton's own view:

> The *things of God* are not made *ours*, by a mere Notion and Speculation; but when they become in us a vital Principle, when they establish in us a State or *temper*, when the things of God are Grounds and Principles of suitable *Operations*.[3]

So Cudworth, in his sermon before the House of Commons, in 1647:

> The Gospell, though it be a Sovereigne and Medicinall thing in itself, yet the mere knowing and believing of the history of it, will do us no good.

Both Cudworth and Whichcote believed with Milton that a mere 'historical' faith is only the

[1] Whichcote : *Moral and Religious Aphorisms*, ed. Inge, 1930, p. 11.
[2] Whichcote : *Collected Works*, Aberdeen, 1751, ii. 95.
[3] Whichcote : *Moral and Religious Aphorisms*, p. 17.

prelude to true faith; that true faith is a more complete and wholly absorbing 'knowledge of spiritual things'.

## IX

As we look back on *De Doctrina Christiana*, can we say that Milton has made for himself a systematic understanding of his Christian belief? Can we be satisfied that on major points no doubts remain and that all the items of his doctrine dovetail together to form a body of opinion well-shaped and coherent? I think not. In too many places, Milton is doubtful of his own conclusions—there is no assurance, for example, in what he has to say of the Holy Spirit; the mystery of the incarnation he will not further discuss; the end of all things is not brought into line with the new thought, for Milton leaves undecided such questions as the destiny of matter, the place of hell, and, for the rest, he makes no departure from orthodox belief. In no part of the treatise does he draw together all the scattered threads of his argument and show their connexion with each other.

There are, however, certain dominating ways of thinking and deep convictions which determine the argument at each point. These have been satisfied individually and atomistically—in the process of satisfaction, Milton has had his eye on a system, much like that of the Cambridge Platonists, but this system has been made up like a mosaic, bit by bit, and it has not grown organically out of a deep philosophical need, it has not shaped and ordered the long argument. The consequence is that, although on each individual point Milton has satisfied some need of his being, he has not satisfied his whole being in the totality of his thought. Man must be free and responsible; and the conception of God as pure will must, in this respect, make an important surrender. The Son as Mediator must be God-Man, and, as God-Man, he cannot be of one essence with the Father; and ideas of triunity, tripersonality, and the like must be dismissed as sophistical notions. Body works up to spirit, and is contained within spirit; all things, therefore, must come out of the substance of God. Man must be thought of as a whole, a living soul: as a whole, therefore, he must suffer death. As we read *De Doctrina Christiana* and *Paradise Lost*, we are not persuaded to a view of God and the universe which is an integration of all these separate ideas. No such view dominates the entire thought. We have the feeling that Milton is still like a man looking about him, still casting about in his mind.

The ideas, the separate convictions that determine the thought and the logic are of different kinds. I should place first what I have called the 'holistic' tendency of Milton's mind. He views the universe as a series of wholes, each total and organic in itself, each merging into and taking part in a larger whole. His view of Christ as one person, in which the divine nature is hypostatically united with the human, arises fundamentally from this habit of mind. His view of man, as a living soul, suffering death in the whole of his nature, has its origin here too. His view of the whole process of things—a simple whole, which is Being, generating out of itself a descending series of beings, themselves wholes, which in their turn return to become one with Being—is as near to an organic philosophical view as Milton anywhere reaches. Milton's anti-Trinitarianism is the product of this 'holistic' view rather than the logical corollary of any system formulated in his mind.

Second is his affection towards God, most difficult, perhaps, of all things in Milton to understand. There can be no doubt that so soon as God ceased to appear as the Deity who had made England and Milton his special charge, God became strange to Milton. In *Paradise Lost*, this strangeness is everywhere apparent. There is a sense in which Milton expresses in *Paradise Lost* his own alienation from God; an alienation which is not the consequence of sin, not the result of any deep feeling of guilt, but which arises from a certain mental perplexity, an inability to make his mind comfortable in belief. *De Doctrina Christiana* affords evidence of this same perplexity. Where the argument expresses Milton's mind most transparently, we feel that he is making an effort to bring God closer to himself, closer to man : to provide for man a more dynamic consciousness of God, a knowledge of God which shall vitalize and sanctify all his conduct. And yet—somehow or other, the effort is not wholly unsuccessful. God remains apart, his nature not adequately known : he is still strange to man. It is, perhaps, in part recognition of this that Milton turns to the Son, makes him something less than supreme God, makes him Mediator as God-Man, truly God and truly Man in one person, suffering death as man suffers death. His difficulty in conceiving God and organizing his affections towards him may in this way have encouraged his anti-Trinitarianism. But he does not give up the attempt to understand the nature of God; he does not resign himself to accept an Absolute which he can never understand. Our faith must be in God: God made the world; God watches over us and his providence preserves the world; in the end, though through Christ, we shall be one with God.

Finally, Milton's deep belief that man is free, that in freedom lies the secret of value and virtue, that man must be held responsible, quickens and transforms his thought. Man must be free: God, then, must be a Being to whom man's free conduct is acceptable and his decrees must be conditional on that conduct. Man is responsible: the ground of our reconciliation with God must, then, be from something in us, not wholly from God's free grace justifying the ungodly. In freedom lies value: faith results in a knowledge of spiritual things which informs our moral judgements and persuades us, of our own free-will, to perform good works. And yet —Milton does not seem to me to be wholly at ease in these views. It is true that in *Paradise Lost* he couples Christian Liberty with the Reason and that in *De Doctrina Christiana* he speaks of conscience, of the rule of the Holy Spirit as 'right reason'. But his view is never thoroughly rational: the purposes of God still remain unknown factors, and to know God, to have faith, is not adequately interpreted as to follow Reason. Man's responsibility before God seems to have been with Milton a more important consideration than man's free competence to perform good works. Man is evermore to blame for his lapses than to be praised for his perseverances.

I do not see how Milton could have been satisfied with *De Doctrina Christiana*. Certainly he seems satisfied in his preface to it—but is it not possible that this was written when Jeremie Picard made his fair copy of the work, when Milton was in no doubt about his intention to publish it ? Is it not possible, too, that although in Jeremie Picard's version there was much unorthodox opinion, Milton's mind moved still farther away from his earlier belief, and radical alterations—made after Picard's first draft was done—put this movement into words ? These alterations seem to have been made after the composition of the earlier books of *Paradise Lost*. The temper in which *Paradise Lost* was written—a certain perplexity of mind and spirit—seems to me to be evident in the treatise. Perhaps *Paradise Regained* and *Samson Agonistes* show a deeper harmony, a mind less troubled.

# THE LATER POEMS

I

O N the later poems, as well as on *Of True Religion*, I base my view that *De Doctrina Christiana* is not an adequate statement of Milton's religious beliefs. *Paradise Regained* is simpler in statement and more direct in meaning than *Paradise Lost*; speculation is more diffident, as though it had given way to limited assurance. In *Samson Agonistes* Milton's spirit is aware of its own troubles, and he makes his peace, as it were, both with God (who is still, perhaps, a little strange to him) and with himself by a self-surrender, self-acceptance which argues rest after much perplexity. In both poems, he returns to Scripture; we have the feeling that, after all, the mind as well as the will has learnt a lesson of obedience.

These poems are better read, not as containing the intellectual fruits of Milton's doctrinal searches, but as expressing the mood that followed when those searches were nearly done, when Milton rested, not perhaps wholly content, but sufficiently serene. It is this serenity, surely, which marks the writing in his last prose work, *Of True Religion*, and which makes him speak so tolerantly of all those sects within Protestantism which held opinions, some of them in agreement, some of them at variance with those he himself expounded in *De Doctrina Christiana*. It is a serenity in which he is prepared to say that 'no man is infallible here on earth' and that the Calvinists are 'not without plea of scripture'.

There are passages in these two poems which make it clear that Milton, though not perhaps in grave doubt as to the truth of his own conclusions, recognized that the Bible is in many points difficult, perhaps doubtful of interpretation, and that, after all, only certain parts of belief are 'necessary to salvation'. In *Paradise Regained*, there is surely a memory of his own experience, when he says:

> he who receives
> Light from above, from the fountain of light,
> No other doctrine needs, though granted true. (iv. 288.)

And in *Samson Agonistes*, the same tale is obliquely told:

> Yet more there be who doubt his ways not just,
> As to his own edicts, found contradicting,
> Then give the rains to wandring thought,
> Regardless of his glories diminution;
> Till by thir own perplexities involv'd,
> They ravel more, still less resolv'd,
> But never find self-satisfying solution. (*S.A.*, 300.)

The ways of God are just and 'justifiable to men'; but who shall say how much of that justification shall end in the simple words: It is not for me to understand, but to obey ?

The pamphlet, *Of True Religion*, seems to me to be written in this mood. When Milton considers the various sects of his time—the Lutherans, the Calvinists, the Anabaptists, and the Arminians—he speaks of their leaders as learned men, anxious to inquire with the assistance of the Holy Spirit, searching all things according to the rule of Scripture. This they have done and this he has done, too. Their disputes, like his (for he names them), have been concerned with things something less than 'necessary to salvation'. It is good that their thoughts should be published without fear of persecution; so that it may be seen by the Papists that Protestant debates are not merely a 'continual wrangle', but a brotherly search after the truth from a common starting-point. Nothing in the pamphlet shows that Milton had either changed his view or abandoned as altogether vain the pursuit of doctrinal truth; but throughout the argument we may read the view that Protestantism is more important than Milton's Christian Doctrine, that 'neighbouring differences' are not enough to rend the church, that all men may err. There is, I am sure, a shift of emphasis.

In these last works, Milton seems to have lost that pride of reason which marks his earlier controversial prose and which, indeed, very often appears in the arguments of *De Doctrina Christiana*. He may well have been still assured in the positions he had taken up; but he is more humble about them. They are not so important, after all—perhaps they have not solved his problem. It is as though he has come to see that reason itself may often be in vain. As he looked back upon his published prose works, his divorce and political pamphlets, he must have been sensible of the fact that much argument is in vain, that in them a great deal of self-assurance had been misplaced. So, too, when his Christian doctrine had been re-formulated, he must have regarded all the laborious argument as something the importance of which had diminished with the years. *De Doctrina Christiana* cannot have been the comfort of his later years, as he had anticipated when he wrote the preface to it. The spirit of the poet could not be consoled by logic and argument.

This change in mood, deepening from *Paradise Regained* to *Samson Agonistes*, accounts for the absence in these two works of any clear mention of that 'system' which lies behind *Paradise Lost* and which is suggested in *De Doctrina Christiana*. Certain beliefs are still assured, but in these poems there is no busy speculation, no mind-searching. There is—chiefly—acceptance, based upon the Scriptures. The conception of God in *Paradise Lost* is doubtful and changing. In these poems, the awareness of God is simpler and more homogeneous. Milton accepts his intuition and puts away argument. *Paradise Regained* is not stirred by any quarrel going on in Milton's mind and spirit. So far as his mind was concerned, at least, the quarrel seems to be done; and the poem lacks a certain energy perhaps because the deeper divisions of the poet's nature are not involved. In *Samson Agonistes*, the mind seems to me to be making its last surrender; but all those deeper divisions are reported and engaged in this last act by which Milton, in the whole of his spirit and not without resistance, became reconciled with his intuition of God.

II

If all that remained to us of Milton's work were *Paradise Regained* and *Samson Agonistes*, we should have an impression of his mind and temper very different from the one given to us by the sum of his works. Where in them is the passion for liberty? Where is the proud belief in Reason, which is also choice? What hint is there in these poems of that kind of 'saving faith' which is argued in *De Doctrina Christiana*?

In *Paradise Regained*, Milton gives a new emphasis to one of the central needs of his nature which had for long lain unrecognized, unadmitted— the need *to obey*. This, I believe, was ultimately more important to him even than liberty: in obedience, rather than in liberty, he came to understand the nature of Christian conduct. This is the end of his search. He had tried to understand the relation between man and God in terms of Christian freedom —he had tried to give to man a spiritual dignity by supposing that the value of his conduct depends partly on his own judgement of what is good and evil, partly on his own 'knowledge of spiritual things'. He had aimed at a more rational faith. These endeavours left him unsatisfied. Still conscious of the terrible power of carnal appetite, still aware of the dangerous blandishments of worldly temptation, knowing still the false pride of reason and the instability of human righteousness, Milton yielded up his sovereignty of understanding and will and rested himself on *obedience*. To obey is best.

This conclusion to his spiritual unrest was the one

most natural to him. Even in his description of Gospel Liberty in *De Doctrina Christiana*, the intellectual assent to the notion of God's goodness working in the human heart is never fired and made alive by any surrender of the whole spirit to the experience of that goodness. It all remains a little too theoretical. Liberty, one feels, appeared to Milton chiefly as a responsibility for evil, not the very condition of good. All this is due, perhaps, to the change worked in Milton's spirit when he could no longer rely on the 'middle sort'—he had believed in freedom and had hoped much of it, but he was disappointed. He blames not God but men; freely they stood who stood and fell who fell. In his deepest being, there must have been an emptiness of spirit in Milton's later years, for, try as he would, the meaning had gone out of freedom and only its responsibility remained. How otherwise shall we interpret *Samson* ?

One part of Milton's outlook has not been sufficiently emphasized—his belief in discipline. He had the poet's love of order and dislike of chaos, and I fancy that a decent serenity in social and domestic life (so long as he himself was not bound and fettered) was of more importance to him than any principle of freedom. This desire for orderliness determines much of his thinking. He shrinks from the anarchy of the passions. He would rather have tyranny than licence. He opposes to Chaos and Confusion the orderly dominion of God. His notion of true liberty, in his earlier works, always contains within it the idea of a rigorous discipline. This is not merely a reasonable self-discipline; it is

14

rather the discipline of one part of the self exercised over others. Conduct, for Milton, is not so much determined by Reason as restrained by Reason, and the commands of Reason are always, in a sense, thought of as coming from outside. He thinks in terms of *serving* Reason, of being *obedient* to its recommendations. In the ultimate analysis, Milton does not think of Reason as enfranchising man's will so much as keeping it on the right lines. This may not be his declared psychology; but it is implicit throughout his thought. When Adam fell, Reason relaxed its control, and the baser appetites achieved the dominion over him. Man's salvation consists very largely in the restoration of a new discipline, the rule of Reason.

*Paradise Regained* tells us of a world saved for God by the Son's refusal to be tempted by the Devil. We see in the figure of the Son Milton's conception of perfect man. It must be confessed that the conception is (mainly perhaps owing to the circumstances of the Temptation) a negative one. In *De Doctrina Christiana*, Milton speaks of that natural reason which enables men to resist bad desires. The Son seems to make that natural reason the mode of true obedience. Every kind of pride and passionate indulgence is resisted because it offers a satisfaction which is not of God. The Son is humble before God and rests himself perfectly on God. It is true that he exercises a kind of reason—he knows that the world is not to be won for God by clash of arms and show of power; he knows, too, that it is indifferent to the salvation of the world that men should have devised for themselves ingenious philosophies. But can it be

said that Milton regards the 'reason of the case' as
the supremely important factor in the Son's decis-
ions ? Surely not. The important decision is one to
obey the Father and not bow down before the Devil.
What the Devil is we know—the Devil is the
symbol for the World and the Flesh, for human
satisfactions and delights. And Reason knows well
enough how to resist these. What the Father is we do
not know—except that he must be obeyed.

The moving moments in *Paradise Lost* are those
in which Milton tells of alienation from God and the
bitter consequences of this alienation. Milton was, I
believe, more hungry for God than for Liberty. In
*Paradise Regained*, the emphasis moves from Liberty
to Obedience. There is a sense in which, notwithstanding the final triumph, it is a pessimistic poem.
Out of the depths of his distrust of the vanity of
earthly things—of reason itself—Milton turned to
obedience and was content to obey where he did not
wholly understand.

*Samson Agonistes* has the quality of a final utter-
ance. Milton composes himself in this poem, settles
his spiritual affairs, and is serene. Once again, there
seems to me to be a profound strain of pessimism in
the poem, and it is this, I think, that has led some
critics to argue that the tone of the poem, its per-
suading atmosphere, is Greek rather than Hebraic.
There is in it a 'grandeur of contrast' between the
ineluctable processes of Fate and the vain heroism of
man. It has the *separate* qualities of Greek tragedy:
it is didactic, religious, serious, and ironical. But
Milton does not side with Samson against Fate or
God—nor do we. We blame Samson even where

we most pity him. We know the agony of mind that follows his alienation from God; but this alienation is something quite foreign to Greek drama. Samson, the chorus, and we ourselves all think of God's service, oneness with God's purposes, as the better, the more blessed way. And Samson's triumph does not affect us as the triumph of the heroic in man, grand though vain. It affects us as the triumph of God through man, grand and purposeful.[1]

Our eyes are on Samson. He is the centre of the play, and in him we read the secret of Milton's spirit. Like Adam, Samson fell through disobedience. Like Adam, too, he surrendered to woman, to the weakness of the flesh. He himself recognizes two kinds of living: that 'strenuous liberty', which is obedience to God, but which is also a continual and watchful resistance to the snares of the flesh; and, on the other hand, the soft and effeminate yielding to women, to wine, and to gluttony. Samson is not merely an heroic victim. He deserves his fate, because he has betrayed his God—he redeems himself by a final heroic service. In the same way, the Philistines deserve destruction—and are not redeemed—for they are soft and self-indulgent and alienate from God.

Most important of all, then, is the intuition of God in *Samson Agonistes*. The poem bears all the marks of having been written by a man who is giving up a search, who is content at last to remain quiet before his intuition of ineffable mystery. The ways of his service we know; but these negatively.

[1] See W. R. Parker, *The Greek Spirit in Milton's 'Samson Agonistes'*, Essays and Studies, 1934.

Him and his ways we cannot fully know, for much in them is unsearchable, much only to be revealed in the processes of time. Milton put aside his puzzlement, his perplexity at what seemed like God's abandonment of his own cause: God's wisdom is 'ever best found in the close'. So many things in this life are patently not of God; so few things are according to his will, that the path of Christian duty is strait and strenuous. Nevertheless, we know enough: we know that we must learn obedience.

This is the end of Milton's long inquiry; and we see in it the source and meaning of all his doubts, his divisions. Passion and pride and false reasoning rule the lives of men. Some glimpses of Reason men still preserve, but its light is flickering and uncertain. Men easily walk in the shadows. Yet God must be; and man must be responsible before him. In *Paradise Lost* and *De Doctrina Christiana*, Milton tried to find a reconciliation between man and God, whereby man's understanding should be illuminated and his will enfranchised by a knowledge of the nature of God, of spiritual things. But this view could not command his deepest assent, for, first, it left too much to the rational judgement of man— and Milton had reason to distrust that—and, secondly, God was in truth still strange to Milton. In *Paradise Regained*, and even more emphatically in *Samson Agonistes*, that strangeness is accepted, and Milton turns to the idea of obedience, away perhaps from the idea of rational co-operation. He comes nearer to the Calvinism which his spirit never utterly rejected. The Calvinist held that God's decrees are unconditioned by anything prior to his pure will. Milton came very near to the view—it is the reverse of the medal—that man's obedience must be unconditioned by anything prior in his understanding and his will. Reason is no longer choice, except in so far as it enables us to resist bad desires. We must learn to obey.